ALIENATION AND ECONOMICS

by Walter A. Weisskopf

THE PSYCHOLOGY OF ECONOMICS

ALIENATION AND ECONOMICS

ALIENATION AND ECONOMICS

Walter A. Weisskopf

E. P. DUTTON & CO., INC.   NEW YORK   1971

To Toni and Alex

Published simultaneously in Canada
by Clarke, Irwin & Company Limited, Toronto and Vancouver

Library of Congress Catalog Card Number: 72-158601
SBN 0-525-05193-7

Preface

In *The Psychology of Economics* [1] I tried to explain certain aspects of economic thought as the result of psychocultural trends: the substitution of a business ethic for the Christian ethic; the substitution of rationalism for a religious interpretation of history and society; the gradual substitution of ethical relativism for a belief in objective values. In a series of subsequent articles I expressed the conviction that economics is largely a normative discipline dealing with the value conflicts of industrial society. I came to the conclusion that this value system can be criticized from the point of view of a philosophical anthropology with a holistic, encompassing image of man and human existence. This critique rests on the assumption that the system of values and reasoning in industrial society neglects essential nonmaterial, intellectual, psychological and spiritual human needs. This book is an elaboration and extension of these ideas.

I want to express my gratitude to Roosevelt University for

----

[1] (Chicago: University of Chicago Press, 1955) and (London: Routledge & Kegan Paul, 1955).

repeated research leaves and teaching load reductions, and to President Rolf A. Weil and Dean of Faculties Otto Wirth for their help and sympathetic understanding. The freedom and the absence of academic orthodoxy at Roosevelt University made it possible for me to remain a "generalist" combining philosophy, psychology and the social sciences and to write this book. I also owe a debt of gratitude to many devoted part-time student assistants for typing a difficult manuscript.

I also want to express my thanks to Marian Skedgell of E. P. Dutton and Company, who, after reading my articles, encouraged me to write this book.

Chicago, February, 1971   Walter A. Weisskopf

Contents

Prologue

I

This book is not a "scientific" discourse but a tract about the philosophy that underlies Western social and economic thinking and acting. It is not "scientific" in the sense that it does not aim at value-neutrality (which I prefer to call value-emptiness) or at detached objectivity; it is critical of these very terms. If it would not sound too presumptuous this book could bear the title "a critique of industrial society," not from an economistic point of view but in the light of philosophical and psychological analysis.

Verities in social thought are not of a universal, time- and space-less nature; truth in human affairs must always be related to a particular historical situation. Universally valid truth, independent of a particular position in time and space, cannot be grasped by human beings because they are finite and conditioned. Although they are able to conceive of the absolute aspect of truth, the truth they can grasp is finite and conditioned. That does not mean that there is no objective validity in social thought; it is "absolutely" true under the explicit and implicit conditions under which it is grasped and expressed. The stress is on the implicit conditions

II

which are often overlooked, because they are not explicitly stated; they include the social, political, psychological and other factors under which these truths were established.

In this sense, a critique of society and of its values does not lack objective validity. It is part of a dialectical historical process. Every given historical reality is a thesis which creates an antithesis. This is so because social existence never encompasses the totality of human nature. Every society permits only certain human propensities to be realized and suppresses others. It bottles up certain drives, inclinations and capabilities which then, like the forces of the unconscious, clamor for realization and bring about social change. The return of the repressed is the psychological basis of critical and utopian thinking. Social critique derives its force from what is repressed under the existing social conditions. It is utopian; a negation of present reality has always been the strongest moving force in history; the turn away from and against reality has been most effective in changing reality.

Thus, a critique of prevalent values is not pure partisanship and subjective evaluation. It is rooted in a historical situation and is subject to experiental (in contrast to experimental) verification. This is verification through an intuitive understanding of the historical process. Such an experiental verification is possible and necessary because man is an observer and, at the same time, a participant in life and history which, for him, is a drama with an unknown content.[1]

Man's role as spectator and participant prevents him from seeing historical reality merely as a detached observer and verifying what he sees through detached objective perception. His perceiving and his acting are mutually interdependent; they change the reality which is perceived and acted upon; this change, in turn, influences and changes perception and action. The totality of this situation is a complex balance of interdependent variables, every one of them cause and effect of the other one. Social critique is based on insight into this process.

However, the question remains: how is critical and utopian

---

[1] Erich Voegelin, *Order and History*, vol. I (Baton Rouge, La.: Louisiana State University Press, 1956), p. 1.

thinking possible? How can we, products and children of our time, being conditioned by our society, transcend the given situation? This is possible because human beings are, at the same time, conditioned *and* free. We are endowed with a certain degree of freedom which enables us to some extent to transcend our conditioning. Such freedom implies a process that psychologists call "dissociation." The individual can transcend himself and reject certain aspects of himself and of his environment.

Social critique is based on a form of self-analysis which, at the same time, is an analysis of the historical situation. It requires penetration into the collective unconscious within oneself. The critic tries to uncover what he and his society repress. Thereby he helps himself and his society to liberate what is repressed.

There is an observable sequence of historical change. First, critical ideas and ideals are developed which reject and negate the existing order and its values and uncover the tendencies repressed by this order which clamor, mostly unconsciously, for liberation. Second, charismatic leaders arise who formulate the new message in such a way that it kindles a fire of new creeds and beliefs among groups of followers. Third, social and political leaders arise who translate these new ideas and ideals into programs of action and form social movements and organizations. Finally, a new social system is realized in new or changed institutions. Then, the entire process repeats itself.

Social critique performs ancillary services, helping the repressed toward liberation; but it has to set in at the pregnant moment, that moment in history when conditions are such that the new can and will emerge from the old. This is the moment when social critique can become fruitful. If this moment has arrived it is time for a broadside attack on most of the cognitive and value presuppositions on which our entire system of scientific, technological and economic rationality rests.

II

The present mood in Western society, especially in the United States, is pessimistic, eschatological, apocalyptic. In the public utterances of the 1960's pessimism more and more replaced the traditional American optimism. A series of events brought this pessimism out into the open. Sputnik, the Bay of Pigs debacle, the assassinations of the Kennedys and of Dr. King, the Vietnam War, the race riots and troubles in the ghettos, militant racism from the right and the left, the various rebellious youth movements and academic revolts, the rediscovery of hunger and poverty, the destruction of the environment, the population explosion, the ravages of urbanization, the nuclear armament race and political instability all over the globe—all this has caused pessimism to creep into even the usually glib and pollyannaish products of the mass media.

However, these events were merely the catalyst which brought a deeper-lying mood to the surface. This mood did not originate in the United States but in Europe after the breakdown of the old order in World War I. Its roots go back to European ideas at the end of the nineteenth and the beginning of the twentieth century. This pessimistic mood was not yet manifest at the end of World War I. On the contrary, it seemed to many that the breakdown of the nineteenth-century order opened the doors for a free society liberated from the fetters of traditional restrictions. However, Western experience since 1918 is best expressed by the slogan "the gods that failed." The gods that failed in the interwar period were political democracy, the free market system, and also communism and socialism. Political liberalism failed in Central Europe and was replaced by the most inhuman totalitarianism of modern times. Economic liberalism failed after World War I and was replaced by economic interventionism and governmental planning almost everywhere in the West. Communism, in the form of Stalinism, disappointed the utopian hopes of many of its followers.

Yet, at the outbreak of World War II the hope for a peaceful and democratic order was still high, at least in the Anglo-Saxon countries. This hope grew dimmer after the end of the war, under the impact of the Cold War, the armaments race, the rivalries between Russia and the United States and the growing gap between the rich and the poor countries. However, pessimism was, at first, confined to the international scene. In domestic affairs, the belief in the welfare state and in democratic institutions was not yet at its ebb. It became almost extinct, however, under the impact of the events of the sixties, at least among a substantial group of intellectuals and among many of the young, and this negative stance has now influenced even the mass media and public opinion.

What was thought to be the greatest strength of Western civilization, science, technology and economic progress, turned out to be Pandora's boxes that threaten this society with destruction. Science helped create nuclear weapons which may for the first time in known history threaten mankind with extinction. The armaments race and increasing sophistication in nuclear, chemical and biological weaponry have moved the unthinkable very close, not only to the thinkable, but to the probable. Medicine, which until recently was considered to be almost wholly beneficial, has helped along the population explosion and raised the specter of overcrowding and mass starvation. Technological and economic progress in combination with urbanization has created the ghettos, traffic congestion, air, water and soil pollution, and disturbed the ecological balances of the natural habitat and of the environment in general. Economic progress did not provide any solution for the problem of poverty, hunger, malnutrition and this not only in the poor countries but even within the fantastically affluent United States. The main institutions of Western society, science, technology and the economy have at least created as many ills as they have remedied.

This experience is tied in with the failure of democratic institutions to carry out even those reforms that seem possible within the existing system. The many measures to improve conditions for the poor, the segregated, the disadvantaged, to integrate the races and achieve equal civil rights seem to have ground to a halt long before their goal was reached. A society mainly motivated by financial self-interest has great difficulty in carrying out altruistic measures; funds destined for the poor and disadvantaged seem to stick too easily to the fingers of those who are supposed to administer such funds. In addition, democracy, with its majority rule, seems unable to render effective help to minorities; and one of the main new facts of this society is that the poor and disadvantaged are, in contrast to all previous societies, a minority.

It is against this background that this book was written. With "the gods that failed" as its leitmotiv, it raises the question of why the gods have failed and why some of them that are still worshiped should be abandoned.

The arguments of this book rest on the assumption that Western civilization suffers from a gigantic repression of important dimensions of human existence. The term repression is related to what theologians call estrangement, and Marxists (and many others today) call alienation. The common link between these concepts is that something that is vital and essential for human life and existence is left out, neglected, suppressed and repressed. Alienation, estrangement and repression imply that human existence is split, that man has been reduced to a part of man, to a part of what man could be.

This repression is the source of our present unrest and uneasiness, and of the mood of pessimistic desperation that permeates life in the West today. All that external events have done is to bring into the open ideas and feeling that have been smoldering under the surface for a long time. But the external events are themselves the result of deep-lying causes, primarily a historical, collective repression of essential human needs, propensities, aspirations and dimensions. This repression is, in large part, due to the *pattern of thought* and the *value-attitudes* which have developed in the West during the last two centuries.

The cause of our predicament is the intellectual and psychological pattern without which our scientific, technical and economic "progress" would not have been possible. This same pattern presupposes that any problems created by external abuses and excesses can be solved with the help of science, technology and the economy. Against this, my thesis is that the root of our ailments lies in this same peculiar rationalism and style of life; the ailments cannot be cured without a profound change in thought and in values.

III

This book deals with alienation and its manifestation in economic thought. It does not deal with what nowadays is called economics, especially not with the methods and techniques used by modern economic analysis, such as mathematics, econometrics, statistics and quantitative model building. The aspect of economics that is of concern here is its value-implications and presuppositions, the implicit assumptions that economists made about the basic motivations, goals, aspirations and ultimate values and meanings of human existence. And even the assumptions of the economists are of interest here only insofar as they express the value-attitudes of their times. The term "economic thought" as used here means the philosophy of life on which economic reasoning and activity during the last two centuries were based. The term "economic philosophy" may be a more appropriate characterization of what is dealt with here.

The social sciences, including economics, are not merely disciplines characterized by subject matter and method. They are self-interpretations of the societies and of the economies from which they emerged. An economic system and the thought about this system stand in the same relation as the actual existence of a person and his consciousness and awareness of this existence: in a relation of mutual interdependence. An economic system and its self-interpretation in economic thought form a whole. The discipline of economics molds into a system what would merely be otherwise an incoherent sequence of external events. The economic system is what its members think it is and economics tells them what to think; but what they think about it is influenced by their experiences within the system which, in turn, depend on how they interpret what they experience as economic reality.

Based on this assumption that economic thought and economic reality reflect and influence each other, it is legitimate to use economic ideas as symptoms of general *value-attitudes*. This term includes all the normative aspects of life in a society: ultimate values which give meaning to life, intermediate values which help in the actualization of the ultimate ones, the way people are supposed to and actually do react to each other and to their experiences—the entire style of life in a society. Economics, or, rather, the moral philosophy which underlies economic reasoning, is a reflection of the prevalent value-attitudes of the period.

The present inclination toward specialization in the social sciences makes it difficult to deal with such integrative topics as alienation and economics. I claim to be a "generalist"—looked on, today, as someone who knows nothing about everything. Although I would like to refute this accusation, there is some truth in it; I cannot claim to be a specialist in all of the fields that are involved in this book. A generalist should see things together which usually are treated as unrelated to each other. Whether this goal has been accomplished only the readers can decide.

I

Alienation and the Structure of Human Existence

EXISTENTIAL ALIENATION

Existential alienation has its roots in the human condition. Man is finite and mortal; he is conditioned by heredity and environment, by his physique, his life history, the accidents of time and place of his birth, and by social and historical factors. But man can transcend the given situation because he is aware of this situation and can look at it as if from the outside. Man "is" and at the same time knows that he is. Through the various forms of his consciousness—thought, language, memory, imagination and vision of the future—he can emancipate himself from what is. He can transcend his position in space: he "is here" but he can imagine what happens somewhere else. He can transcend his position in time by remembering what was and by imagining the possibilities of the future. He can transcend the immediate sensory experience by his conceptual thought.

This transcendence of the immediately given experience is the source and the cause of existential alienation. Through his consciousness man is alienated from his world and his world is alienated from him.

Human existence has a polar structure; it is split into a self and a world which "reflects the subject-object structure of being which in turn presupposes the self-world structure as the basic articulation of being. The self having a world to which it belongs—this highly dialectical structure—logically and experientially precedes all structure." [1] What Tillich means to say is that when we perceive the world, when we think and talk about the world, about reality, we usually abstract from the inevitable fact that this situation always presupposes a perceiving, thinking, talking subject and a perceived thought-about, talked-about object. To us, reality is always split into a subject-object structure, into self and world whether we are, at the moment, aware of it or not. When we see a tree, the tree is not a detached object but part of a dichotomic, subject-object structure. The total phenomenal reality is composed of the tree and of the "I" that perceives it. The entire structure of our world is dichotomic.

This causes existential alienation. If we concentrate on what is outside of us, on the world, we are split off from ourselves as the subject. If we concentrate on ourselves as the subject, we are split off from the world. We are unable to avoid this dichotomy except in rare "peak experiences": in mystic trances, in sexual and sensual ecstacies, in those "flashes of understanding in which the mind is flooded with light" (Plato, Seventh Letter). This split is the basis of eros in the broadest sense, the longing to unite what is separated. Most human striving for a state of ultimate bliss, happiness, Nirvana, fulfillment of whatever kind, aims at the union of these split opposites. In one way or another, men strive to overcome this split by overcoming the separating effects of consciousness.

They try to escape this split by union downward or union upward. Both aim in different ways to overcome consciousness. Union downward tries to eliminate consciousness through such means as intoxication, drug addiction (which is not an expansion but an extinction of consciousness), sexual stupor, apathetic passivity, "through wine, woman and song," on the sensual level. The movements of today which use massage, nudism, sensitivity train-

---

[1] Paul Tillich, *Systematic Theology*, vol. I (Chicago: University of Chicago Press, 1951), p. 164.

ing, physical touch encounters, and so forth are trying to find ways to overcome, by more or less physical means, the estrangement from which we suffer. Sometimes definite elements of union upward, with expansion of consciousness, are involved in these activities. Aldous Huxley's mysticism, built on mescaline, is a mixture of both.

Union upward is the attempt to overcome the split between self and world without the extinction of consciousness, a synthesis of self and world. Union downward negates consciousness; union upward affirms it. Such values as truth, beauty and love are goals of union upward. Knowledge of truth is brought about by an eros which unites the knower with the known.[2] It shows clearly the pattern of separation and alienation and the path toward union and synthesis: a detached knowing center unites itself with the object of knowledge without destroying the detachment. Modern scientific and technological knowledge, with its alleged value-neutrality, overstresses detachment and therefore by negating intuition and tacit knowledge fails to unite the knower with the known. But the creative and re-creative experience of beauty involves a situation in which the viewer and creator merge and become one with the beautiful object without destroying the subject and the object of artistic creation or experience. Love relations are the deepest and most satisfying way to overcome the self-world split. It requires a full and unlimited affirmation of the world, represented by the other, the Thou, and the union with the other without either submission or destruction of either the I or the Thou. In all these situations the basic pattern is the same: subject and object are united in a higher synthesis without being extinguished in the process.

In the structure of human existence, subject and object are antinomic but polar; they are interdependent; one cannot be without the other. This polarity implies that the two branches of the antinomy are two aspects of the same totality. This trinity of subject, object and synthesis is most lucidly symbolized by the Yin–Yang sign in Chinese philosophy, by the two intertwined halves in black and white, included in the union of the circle. This symbol not

---

[2] *Ibid.*, pp. 94 ff.

only represents the basic pattern of alienation but shows the way to overcome it: namely by a union or a balance between the two branches of the antinomy.

Existential alienation is caused also by the separation between actuality and potentiality in human existence. Consciousness enables man to grasp potentialities. He can envision what is not, but could be. Man is finite, mortal and aging, limited in time and space, and can actualize only a few of his potentialities. At the same time he is gifted or cursed with the ability to envision the unactualized possibilities because of his ability to transcend the limits of his existence in his mind. His finitude prevents him from realizing all of his potentialities; but his consciousness and transcendence let him see those potentialities. This creates what one could call a Tantalus situation. Man can grasp the potential but is confined to the actual. There is, in human existence, a continuous conflict between the wide realm of envisioned possibilities and the limited realm of actuality.

Transcendence through consciousness and the grasping of potentialities are the basis of human freedom and free choice. Man could not choose if he could not transcend the given situation and envision alternative possibilities. With such consciousness and transcendence he can envision alternatives between which he can and has to choose. By transcending the given situation through his consciousness, man frees himself—within certain limits—from the necessities of this situation; he can choose between the alternatives grasped by transcending consciousness.

It is a matter of one's temper whether one sees this ability to choose and this freedom as a blessing or a curse. One does not have to be the ass of Buridanus or an indecisive neurotic to see that every choice and decision entails the *sacrifice* of alternatives which have been rejected. The finite conditioned nature of man requires choices between alternative possibilities because not all of them can be realized under given conditions. Once a choice is made all other alternatives have become impossible. One hour devoted to work cannot also be devoted to lovemaking. Once a career is chosen it is difficult to change to another one, and even in our flexible society the number of careers that can be realized in a lifetime is limited. Thus, man is free mostly to renounce possibilities.

This is the existential ground of what economists call scarcity and costs. The scarcity principle implies that in the human situation means of production and need satisfaction are always scarce in relation to needs and ends which are unlimited and can never fully be satisfied. Therefore there is a continuous gap between means and ends which justifies the goal of never-ending economic growth. It will be shown that this idea as applied in economics is historically relative and culture-bound and represents the special orientation of industrial society toward economic activity and material need satisfaction. There is, however, a sense in which the scarcity principle is universally valid because it is rooted in the conditions under which human beings exist. Existential scarcity is caused by human finitude on the one hand, and by the human ability to transcend this finitude and the given existential condition through consciousness and thought on the other hand. This situation shows all the characteristics of the scarcity principle as applied in economic thought. The two principles can be distinguished as *economic* versus *existential scarcity*. Both lead to an allocation problem of scarce means to alternative ends. Both involve the sacrifice of alternative potentialities which are the cost of any definite concrete allocation.

Human life is confronted with an allocation problem not only in respect to material means of production. The resources which are ultimately scarce are *life*, *time* and *energy* because of human finitude, aging and mortality. It is possible that, if we were immortal and if we had eternal youth so that our energy would never decline, no allocation problem and no problem of choice between, or conflict of, goals would exist. We could realize all of our ends one after another with unflagging energy and without any problem of economizing time or energy. There is, however, a question whether allocation and economizing and decisions about preferences may not have to be made even with immortality and eternal youth as long as we are subject to the limitations of time and space; whatever our situation, we can actualize only limited desires here and now, and never all desires at the same time and at the same point in space; we have to leave the others to future satisfaction. However, with immortality and eternal youth, this postponement may be less burdensome than it is under present conditions where a choice may involve the sacrifice of gratification during our lifetime and thus forever.

Talk about immortality and eternal youth is, of course, merely thinking the unthinkable and imagining the unimaginable; it is purely utopian fiction. It is hard to believe in the fulfillment of this wish dream in spite of all predictions about the progress of medicine. It is more likely that any progress in accomplishing longevity would merely change our elder citizens into vegetables and not into Olympian gods (as Aldous Huxley has described it in *After Many a Summer Dies the Swan*).

Because we are mortal and aging, we are confronted with existential scarcity. This scarcity stems, however, not merely from our finitude and mortality but from the *combination* of our finitude with our awareness of possibilities. Finitude, mortality, being confronted with limited conditions alone does not create scarcity; it is merely a problem of adjustment to the limiting environment and of survival. All animals have this problem which they solve by instinct with no, or few, choices between alternatives. The special human problem which makes alienation unavoidable is that, although we also have to survive and to adjust, we know that there are alternatives and that we have to choose between them, knowing that this means sacrifice and renunciation. It is consciousness, knowledge, the freedom and the necessity of choice and the awareness of the sacrificed alternatives which generate the experience of alienation.

This, then, is the existential root of the idea of scarcity and the real foundation of the economic concepts of limited means and unlimited ends. Economists are wont to define their discipline as dealing with the problems of allocation of scarce means toward alternative ends, assuming that the means are always scarce whereas the ends are always unlimited and thus require allocation and economizing of means. The means that are existentially limited are life, time and energy; the ends are not literally unlimited, but they consist of all the potentialities which are dormant in the actual situation and can be envisaged but not realized because of the finite human condition.

✓ This finitude and this limitation exist in spite of human freedom which is conditioned freedom. Man is not free to choose between any alternatives that come to his mind; his freedom is not arbitrary and infinite. He can only choose between the possibilities which are within his reach, determined by the conditions of his existence, such as his physiology, his life history, education and social environment. The person who is free is a conditioned and limited person. Therefore, the potentialities are not unlimited in the strict sense: a person may have the wish dream of being a great general, whereas his genes and upbringing enable him to become an artisan, a farmer or a salesman. The individual has to make a choice, not between infinite possibilities but between those that are preformed in his personality. Thus, man is free to decide between those potentialities that are within his reach but unrealizable within one lifetime. This is the basic meaning of economizing.   ✓

That freedom of choice and decision exists within the limits of personality and of the conditioned self is not alienation but an existential datum. What constitutes existential alienation is that man can only actualize certain selected potentialities and must necessarily sacrifice others which are also within the limit of his personality. He could actualize them, but having made a choice he has sacrificed them. This is alienation because he thus becomes alienated from some of his own potentialities.

The conclusion is that alienation cannot be completely eliminated. Being human is being alienated. Under no circumstances can man accomplish an existence in which he can actualize all of his potentialities. Those psychologists who have preached self-actualization as the supreme goal in life (Erich Fromm, A. H. Maslow) have overlooked the inevitability of existential alienation caused by human conditioning, finitude and mortality. They overlook that man has to renounce many potentialities because they are incompatible with his actual mode of life. Renunciation and its inevitable consequence, suffering, are essential characteristics of human existence. To deny this is to raise hopes which can never be fulfilled and lead only to disillusion, despair and self-destruction. Nothing has been more pernicious in human history than the raising of utopian hopes which are incompatible with the conditions of human existence. The lack of realism and intellectual honesty about what is possible in human affairs is the most potent cause of nihilism.

However, the advocates of self-realization may have in mind something different from what they are actually saying. They may mean that man can and should actualize more, and different, potentialities than those which he is actualizing in modern society. This is the main theme of this book and the basis of its critique of economics and the economy.

Where part of human potentialities are excluded from realization, man needs *guiding norms* for choice and decisions. The Biblical story of the Fall shows in symbolic language the interrelation of knowledge and ethics. The serpent promised "eritis sicut deus scientes bonum et malum" (you will be like God knowing good and evil). This is another way of saying that consciousness and knowledge created the split between the actual and the potential and that this knowledge requires guiding norms for decisions, that is, knowledge of what is good and what is bad. Thus, ethics and morality are not merely epiphenomena and superstructures of the physical and of the actual, but the normative dimension is an essential characteristic of human existence. The creature called man knows that there are alternatives; he is confronted with the problem of choice. Choice requires a standard for choosing, that is, moral and ethical norms.

The content of these norms is largely determined by society. However, it should be well understood that the normative is more than a social category. What we consider right and wrong may be influenced by social mores and attitudes; but the moral is a dimension of existence and not merely a social product. The normative dimension rests on consciousness, knowledge of alternatives, transcendence of the given situation and the necessity of choice—conditions which exist apart from society. This is not a metaphysical assumption but a phenomenological datum of human existence. Morality and the normative are rooted in the human predicament created by human knowledge of alternatives.

Norms are necessary to make choices, and choices always involve sacrifice. This is the root of the experience of compulsion and restriction which is inherent in the moral act, whether the moral rule is imposed from the outside or by the individual on himself. The application of a moral rule always implies that one part of the personality is set against another part, because man knows that he sacrifices some of his potentialities when making a decision.

The relation between facts and values, between the "is" and the "ought to," has been endlessly discussed in philosophy, especially after Kant opened up the abyss between pure and practical reason. There can be little doubt that logically an "ought to" cannot be derived from an "is." Because things are as they are does not prove that they are as they should be or that they should be different from what they are. However, in a deeper sense, any belief in values must ultimately be rooted in an existing structure. In the great belief systems which have influenced human history, the belief in what ought to be was always ultimately derived from a belief in what is. Moral commands were traced back to God, to nature, to reason, to innate instincts and so forth. In spite of the *logical* antinomy between the "is" and the "ought to," the experienced validity of the norm must ultimately rest on a belief system, an image and an interpretation of the universe, of nature and society. This is another way of saying that the normative is an essential aspect of the totality of human existence. It also means that the "is" and the "ought to" may be *logically* distinct but are *psycho-logically* interdependent. Man cannot believe in the validity of an ethical norm without the conviction that this norm is part of the structure of being.

The question of values, and of value-relativism and its alienating effects in modern society, will be discussed again, especially in relation to economics (see pp. 43 ff.). Suffice it to say at this point that norms and values, in order to influence human action, must contain an absolute element. One has to distinguish between the formal absoluteness of the moral imperative on the one hand, and the relativity of its contents on the other hand. ". . . the absolute character of the moral imperative . . . means if something is demanded from us morally, this demand is an unconditional one. The fact that the contents of the moral imperative change according to

one's situation in time and space does not change the formal absoluteness of the moral imperative itself." [3]

This distinction is of the utmost importance. Our present
nihilism of values stems from the confusion of the absolute form
of the moral imperative and the relativity of its content. This confusion has been caused by instrumental, scientistic reason which has
no understanding for the normative as a special dimension. The
scientistic approach sees only the facts of valuation and the multi-
farious changes of the content of values during the course of
history. The inner experience of the unconditional demand of the
moral imperative escapes the limited vision of instrumental, factual,
scientistic reason. Only the changing content of norms is perceived
and the experience of the absoluteness is overlooked. In human
affairs the validity of a cognitive or of a moral principle is always
limited by the conditions implied in the principle. Even the principles of Newtonian physics are valid only under certain conditions, and those of quantum mechanics and relativity theory under
other conditions. Nevertheless both systems are valid and true
under the limiting conditions which are part of the system. The
same thing is true of a moral imperative: it claims absolute validity
under limiting conditions: thus, in our present moral code, murder
is forbidden but killing in self-defense, juridical and military
killing are permissible.[4] The validity of cognitive or normative
statements is always "absolute" under the implied conditions. No
statement, normative or cognitive, can ever be of such an absolute
validity that it is valid under any and all conditions *in abstracto*
(with the exception of certain ontological statements that apply to
being as such); this is inherent in the specificity and circumscribed
nature of all but ontological statements. Even the statement "two
times two is four" is conditioned by the principles inherent in the
structure of mathematics within which it is expressed.

In respect to moral imperatives this combination of formal
absolute validity and relativity of content (or absolute validity combined with relativizing conditions) is sometimes confused with the

---

[3] Paul Tillich, *My Search for Absolutes* (New York: Simon & Schuster, 1967),
pp. 93 ff.
[4] *Ibid.*, p. 99.

question of purely subjective versus interpersonal validity. Are moral norms merely valid for one individual under certain given conditions or can they also be valid for a group? This is an entirely different question from the one of the absoluteness of the moral imperative. There are valid norms for groups of people under common conditions. This situation is not different from the validity of a moral imperative for one person; in both cases the absolute validity is circumscribed by its conditions; if they are present for all members of a group the moral imperative has validity for each member of a group as an individual.

For those for whom the distinction between the formal absoluteness of the moral imperative and the relativity of its content is too dialectical to be grasped, the psychological argument has to suffice: it is quite impossible to believe in and to orient one's action by values unless one believes in their absolute validity for oneself *under the given conditions*. The moral imperative must be experienced as having an absolute claim on oneself, that is absolute validity; otherwise it is degraded to a matter of taste or whim or to a matter of social compulsion. A principle is not a moral one unless it is felt to have an absolute claim on those to whom it is addressed. This is the psychological experiential basis of the philosophical insight that moral norms have a formal absolute character.

The same idea can also be expressed in symbolic religious language: only God knows and embodies the ultimate truth and the ultimate good. Man, in his finite imperfection, does not share this knowledge; but he must act with the conviction that there "is" an ultimate truth and an ultimate good, and that he has to try to reach it, however asymptotically. Man cannot become God but he has to try to do so in spite of the knowledge that this is impossible. This is the inescapable tragedy of the human situation.

In more pragmatic terms this implies that we must have the courage of our convictions and act as if they had an absolute validity but keep in mind that we may be wrong. The problem is to avoid the extremes of rigidity in respect to the content of our values on the one hand, and mere expediency about values on the other hand. The insight into the formal absoluteness of the moral imperative helps us to avoid the latter, the recognition of the relativity of the content of values to avoid the former. As in all human affairs this is a question of balance and not a question of either-or.

Norms, moral and ethical rules, have a social matrix; they are mostly promulgated by society. The individual lives within a group, society and culture which determines his relations to himself, to others and to the world around him. His feeling, willing and thinking, his language, his perception of reality, indeed his very concept of what reality is, is largely determined by the value-attitude system of society.

Values and attitudes range from conscious ultimate ends and beliefs in the meaning of life to the ways of interaction which determine the behavior of people and what they expect from each other. Value-attitudes include what individuals will die for and what they do when they meet each other for the first time. They are the real substance of society and of interaction. Social institutions are not external objects, but consist of value-attitudes which regulate interpersonal relations. For example, the institution of private property means that people expect others to behave in a certain way in respect to the things they own: protection from theft, actions of police and courts, and so forth. Social institutions then consist in value-attitude systems which determine behavior and expectations of behavior.

Value-attitude systems can be conscious, preconscious or unconscious. Ultimate values and values underlying crucial choices and decisions which involve life and death, choices of careers, marriage and so forth are mostly made on the basis of consciously held values. Preconscious values are those which the individual is not aware of when he makes a decision but which could be made conscious at any time; this applies especially to habitual and routine behavior.

The concept of unconscious value systems has been developed by depth psychology. It assumes that men are not guided by consciously adopted norms only but also by normative systems which become unconscious and internalized and thus guide behavior without any conscious knowledge of the actor.

Through identification, introjection and internalization, social norms and values become a part of the individual psyche. They induce the individual to make the choices which society requires him to make. What happens is that (1) normative rules, values and attitudes of social origin are internalized and become part and parcel of the individual's personality. (2) These internalized normative systems can become partly or wholly unconscious and influence a person's thought, feeling and action without his being aware of it. (3) The internalization of such systems of values and attitudes is a process which enables the individual to conform in his thoughts, feelings and actions to the demands of society. It facilitates his doing what he is expected to do by society and his fulfilling his social role. (4) Such internalized normative systems, in spite of the fact that they are part of an individual's psychical apparatus, have a supraindividual, collective content and a continuity in time. The value systems of the parents mold those of the children. Although the children may be in rebellion against the parental values, they are still influenced by the values of the parents. Kenneth Keniston believes that the present-day activists among the students are not in rebellion against parental values but "are concerned with living out expressed but unimplemented parental values." [5] Members of the same group, society and subculture have internalized value systems with the same content, although with individual variations. Such an internalized value system is an unconscious, half- or preconscious part of an individual's character structure molded by social influences and representing internalized social norms.

The social value-attitude system is not identical with the totality of human nature and of the total personality. There are human traits, inclinations, propensities, ways of thinking, feeling, willing, acting, which are not included in the socially accepted style of life. The relation between the totality of "human nature" and

---

[5] Kenneth Keniston, "The Sources of Student Dissent," *Journal of Social Issues,* XXIII (July 3, 1967), p. 119.

personality on the one hand and the prevailing social value-attitude system on the other hand, can be represented in the form of a larger concentric circle (the total personality) in which a smaller circle is contained (the socially acceptable value-attitude system). The total personality is more inclusive than the socially accepted one. From this it follows that there is always a "part" of the human personality which cannot be actualized in any society, or if so, only with great difficulties.

Thus, a condition of antinomy arises between the human traits and propensities which society permits to become real and actual, and potentialities which are neglected, suppressed and repressed. A dichotomy arises between manifest and hidden traits and human proclivities, propensities and goals.

This situation is the *social* root of alienation, which is only a part of the existential alienated situation of man. It is a special form of existential alienation. Alienation in whatever form consists in estrangement from parts of the human personality. Alienation has often been interpreted as alienation from society only; more and more subcultures consider themselves to be alienated from present Western society. This is true only on the surface. Alienation takes place within the individual personality although it can be caused by social factors. The groups who consider themselves and are considered by others to be alienated from society suffer either from the fact that some of their personality traits cannot be actualized in the existing social system or from the fact that they are not even allowed to actualize the personality traits which conform to the value system of their society. In both cases it is *self-alienation which underlies alienation from society*.

It may be possible to distinguish between degrees of a social alienation and to relate them to class structure. One could range the various subgroups in a society according to the degree to which they have successfully internalized the values of their society and realized these values in their mode of life. Those who are highest on this scale and are most identified with the social value system belong to the "elite." The further away a group is from embodying the values of society, the further it is removed from the elite. This psychological situation is the basis of power, wealth, status and self-respect in a society. As long as the basic values are embraced and deeply rooted in the minds of individuals, the value system and the social hierarchy on which it is built will be relatively stable; authority will be legitimized. As soon as the value system begins to disintegrate for whatever reasons, the social hierarchy and the class stratification begin to be questioned. The groups remote from the old value system will begin to clamor for a higher status. This is what the proletariat did and what the disadvantaged groups are doing today.

ⅩBELIEF SYSTEMS, REASON AND ALIENATION

Social values and the repression which they imply are supported by central belief systems, in a world outlook which unifies cognitive and normative beliefs in an interpretation of reality (the universe, society and the self). This central world outlook makes the manifest reality comprehensible and meaningful; at the same time it legitimizes social institutions and the rule of the governing elite by "a world philosophy that organized the universe and men into some sort of satisfactory coherent meaningful whole." [6] For instance, in the high Middle Ages, Thomistic rationalism legitimized and justified a religious belief system and social institutions. Reason, uniting facts and values, performed a legitimizing function; it confirmed the status quo. This was a stable cultural situation because beliefs and reasons were mutually supporting each other and served to alleviate the burden of social and existential repression.

This stability is endangered when reason becomes separated from the central world outlook and the social value system. This is the stage of *critical reason* in distinction from the stage of *conforming reason*. Critical reason turns against the existing value system. In this stage social repression is no longer supported by the central world outlook and its belief system. Reason and belief part ways. Then, repression, deprived of its rationalization, becomes intolerable and the repressed forces clamor for realization.

This is a complex and subtle process. It is not merely that the

---

[6] A. H. Maslow, *Motivation and Personality* (New York: Harper & Brothers, 1954), p. 88.

belief system loses its power over the minds of people, and then the repressed forces begin to surge to the surface: the two movements are mutually interdependent. The repressed forces undermine the belief system and the weakening of the belief system liberates the repressed forces; both movements take place at the same time. The link between the two is the reasoning ego; through criticism it undermines the belief system and, at the same time, becomes conscious of the repressed forces and acknowledges them as a part of the total personality.

The distinction between conforming and critical reason is related to the idea of natural law which emerges at a stage of civilization in which there is a need for a critical approach to the social order. It involves a search for a higher category, over and above the social value system and its institutions, from which their legitimacy can be rationally derived or attacked. The common link between conforming and critical reason, if it appears in the form of natural law, is that there is such a higher dimension over and above the existing cognitive, normative and institutional system. Natural law can then be conforming or confirming; in this case it serves to legitimize and justify the existing order; this is what Karl Mannheim called an ideology. Such a natural law ideology is not simply a submission to and acceptance of the existing order; it is a rationalization of this order, and it emerges because there is a need for such a rationalization. The existing order is no longer unquestionably accepted. Its legitimacy has to be derived rationally from a higher instance; but in the case of conservative, ideological natural law, this higher instance is used to justify the existing order by arriving at the conclusion that its cognitive, normative and institutional aspects are rooted in the natural order of things. The free market ideology became, during the nineteenth century, such a confirming ideology.

In its *critical* form natural law becomes a utopia. It develops a cognitive, normative and institutional system which is different from the existing one and uses it to attack the existing order. This was the original meaning of individualistic democracy and of the free market ideology. At their outset they both were critical utopias directed against the existing order of monarchic and aristocratic rule and against the mercantilistic regulations and restrictions of the economy.

A third stage appears with the prevalence of technical rationality, which is content- and value-empty, concerned only with means, not ends, and devoid of any natural law and any normative, ideological or utopian substance. It is neither confirming nor critical reason. This is the characteristic mode of social thought that developed in the late nineteenth century in the West.

To summarize:

1. The basic split in human existence caused by consciousness is the source of what one can call existential alienation. Alienation is akin to what Christian theology calls estrangement, and to what Freud calls repression. It implies that certain aspects, traits, inclinations, drives and potentialities of man are cut off from realization. Thus human existence is split in two, into a manifest and into a hidden sphere; one actualized, the other suppressed.

2. No society, culture or historical period, nor any human person can be free of alienation. The structure of alienation is determined by the social value-attitude system, supported by central beliefs which make alienation and repression meaningful and bearable. The aspects of the human person which are suppressed in a particular society vary; and it is possible to change the content of alienation by changing the value-attitudes, belief systems and institutions of any society. Social change consists of just such a development in which what was previously suppressed and alienated becomes the predominant feature of the new society.

3. This approach rests on a philosophy of balance between opposing forces in the human person and in society. There is an antinomy between what is manifest and what is hidden and repressed in human existence and in social life. Change in history is propelled by the attempt to establish a balance between two opposing forces, to reunite what has been separated. But ultimate harmony and the union of opposites is impossible within the limits of human finitude and within history. What is possible, however, is to remedy the particular and specific alienating conditions within a given society and at a given historical moment if the conditions are ripe for a change.

2

Alienation and Repression in Western Civilization

The concepts of existential and social alienation can be applied to Western civilization, that is, the society, economy and culture which has developed in England, Western Europe and North America during the last two hundred years. This period is characterized by a series of gigantic repressions: the repression of certain aspects of reason; the repression of the normative dimension; the repression of drives and emotions (impulse control). These repressions involve alienation from certain dimensions and aspects of human existence:

1. The reduction and restriction of reason to reasoning, or the repression of encompassing, existential, substantial reason in favor of technical, instrumental, formalized, content- and value-empty reason and means-ends rationality.

2. The elimination of the normative, of values, of morality and ethics as a dimension of life and thought.

3. The repression of drives, passions, emotions, feelings, sentiments, sensuality, sensuousness, sensitivity; of fantasy, spontaneity, creativity, joy, play, nonpurposive, expressive behavior; all this we shall summarize under the term "impulse control."

THE DEMOTION OF REASON
AND THE REPRESSION OF MORALITY

It is customary to look at the last four hundred years of Western history as a period of liberation and progress. Science, technology, the industrial and market system, the so-called increase in the standard of living, urbanization, and so forth are usually interpreted as advances toward a better life, in spite of the fact that during the last few decades awareness of the detrimental effects of these developments has increased and today attention has turned more and more to the deficiencies of the system. Still, such deficiencies are considered "externalities" not inherent in the system itself. It is assumed that they can be remedied by the very institutions which have caused them. Only in fringe groups does the conviction seem to have taken hold that nothing short of revolutionary change can cure these ailments. This is what the fight between the new radicals and the old liberals is about. Regardless of one's stand in this fight, it is hard to deny that there are crucial elements in modern Western civilization which undermine it from within; its ailments are not externalities but are caused by an entire mode of life and thought. One way to view the development of the West is as a long period of disintegration from a stable culture with a firmly established central world outlook protecting its values and institutions and containing its repressions. In this view the pivots on which Western society rests have become rotten and are in danger of collapse. One of the causes of this development is that an antinomy within reason developed in Western culture and in industrial society. The unity of reason was destroyed and reason was split in two. This dichotomy has been expressed in various terms: reason versus intellect, "Vernunft versus Verstand," objective versus subjective reason, ontological versus technical reason. This latter distinction is, according to Paul Tillich, the result of a historical development. "According to the classical philosophical tradition, [ontological] reason is the structure of the mind which enables the mind to grasp and to transform reality. It is effective in the *cognitive, aesthetic, practical* and *technical* function of the human mind. . . . In the concept of *technical* reason, reason is reduced to the capacity for *reasoning*. Only the *cognitive* side of the classical concept of reason remains, and within the cognitive realm only these cognitive acts which deal with the discovery of *means* for ends." [1] The main difference between ontological and technical reason is that the first encompasses all of human activity, not only the cognitive activity. "Even emotional life is not irrational in itself and subject to the application of reason. This application requires eros, intellectual love, appetitus that drives the mind towards the true and the good." [2] In view of the all-inclusive nature of ontological reason I call it *encompassing reason*. It is not confined to certain spheres or realms of human existence; all of them, including the passions, emotions and feelings, have a rational, a logos-structure.

Encompassing and technical reason (reasoning) are complementary and form a whole. This is of special importance in relation to the distinction between ends and means. Encompassing reason applies to ends as well as means. "While reason in the sense of Logos [ontological reason] determines the ends and only in the second place the means, reason in the technical sense determines the means while accepting the ends from 'somewhere else.' " In industrial society technical reason (reasoning) has been separated from ontological reason. "The consequence is that the ends are provided by non-rational forces. . . . Critical reason has ceased to exercise any controlling forces over norms and ends." [3]

Thus a reduction of reason, a reduction of the whole to one of its parts has taken place. Encompassing reason, applicable to all human activities and functions, including feeling, passion, emotions, aesthetic pursuits and practical action, has been narrowed down to pragmatic utilitarian reasoning about appropriate means for extrarationally given ends. It is exclusively *expedient rationality*. ". . . that kind of conduct in which the actor seeks to attain values by means regarded as conforming to principles of economy of effort, efficiency, and absence of undesirable conse-

---

[1] Tillich, *Systematic Theology*, vol. I, pp. 72 ff.
[2] *Ibid.*, p. 72.
[3] *Ibid.*, p. 73.

quences." [4] This took place in two steps: one, reduction of reason to the cognitive sphere only; and two, reduction of reason to the choice of appropriate means and exclusion of rationality from the realm of norms, ends and values.

Technical reason is dominant in the fields of natural science, technology and in economics. Technical reason is identical with what is commonly called rationality. The reduction of encompassing reason to technical reason was and is a process which transcends economics; its manifestation in the economy is only a special form of a general development in Western civilization.

Max Horkheimer has analyzed this development.[5] His distinction between objective and subjective reason is identical with Tillich's distinction between ontological and technical reason. Objective reason is applicable to ends, goals, emotions, ideals and norms. Subjective reason excludes all these from its universe of discourse and confines itself to the choice of means for extrarational given ends. Objective reason is not pure form but has a substance; its judgments have a specific content; subjective reason is completely formalized and empty of substantial content. Thus, the dichotomy of objective-subjective reason coincides with the one of substantive and formalized reason. The process of disintegration of objective, substantial, encompassing, ontological reason started with the divorce of philosophy from mythology, religion and theology that took place in the West beginning in the sixteenth century. Rationalist philosophy during the seventeenth and eighteenth centuries, although it rejected the authority of revelation as irrational, still retained a *substantial* content in its concept of reason. It secularized Christian beliefs, especially Christian ethics, and considered its directives as the result of substantive, ontological objective reason. Political ideals such as justice, equality, happiness, democracy and freedom were based on reason, natural law, and considered as self-evident *truth*. These ideals were derived by applying reason to nature and society. Political democracy and the free market system were considered to be

[4] Howard Becker, *Through Values to Social Interpretation* (Durham, N.C.: Duke University Press, 1950), p. 23.
[5] In *The Eclipse of Reason* (New York: Oxford University Press, 1947).

justifiable by reason. Classical economics retained a belief in objective, ontological reason. Normative thinking was still considered as part of rational thinking during the Enlightenment. The pioneers of bourgeois civilization founded their ideas and ideals on objective reason.

In the development of industrial civilization during and after the nineteenth century, the remaining traces of objective reason were gradually eliminated; encompassing reason was more and more reduced to technical reason. The formalization of reason gradually emptied it of its content. It became an instrument for nonrational ends and surrendered to a heteronomous content.

This formalization, relativization and subjectivization resulted in the replacement of the ideals of the individualistic, democratic and free market society by the concepts of individual self-interest, and of rule by the majority. The idea that there are objective standards of truth and goodness, comprehensible through reason, was abandoned. Reason "was harnessed to the social process . . . and assumed purely 'operational value.' " Thinking became "part of the process of production." [6] If society has only the function to realize the satisfaction of individual self-interests regardless of their content, society is reduced to a mechanism which coordinates the "random ends" and the "irrational" pursuits of individuals. By abandoning the judgments of objective reason, society becomes a machine which can coordinate any ends, good or bad. Thus reason has abdicated as a guide to a rational choice of goals and becomes a pragmatic instrument. Reason and ends are subjectivized, relativized and formalized. This manifested itself in the relativistic concept of democracy and in the relativistic interpretation of the free market.

This trend can be seen in the changing meaning of the majority principle. Originally, it had an objective content and rested on objective reason. The original idea behind the majority principle was that objective reason is the basis of self-evident truth from which commonsense concepts are derived. The majority will come to a decision not through compromise of individual interests

---

[6] *Ibid.*, p. 70.

but on the basis of reason accessible to every human being. The idea "vox populi, vox dei" was secularized in the idea that the voice of the majority would reflect the voice of objective reason. Later, the majority principle was interpreted as a purely relativistic device of expediency: "deprived of its rational foundation [in objective reason] it has assumed a completely irrational aspect." [7]

We shall see that this interpretation underlies some economic theory about the free market and consumers' sovereignty and has recently been challenged by raising moral questions in economics. The same relativistic, subjectivistic and pragmatic interpretation began to permeate political theory. In a famous essay which had the greatest impact in Central Europe in the interwar period, Hans Kelsen maintained that value-relativism is the basis of democracy. In democracy, Kelsen maintains, all political opinions and movements must be equally respected; "even the opposite opinion must be considered as possibly true if one abandons the idea of an absolute value." [8] According to Kelsen, value-relativism is the essence of democracy; belief in the objective validity of norms or values and in an objective distinction between the good and the bad is incompatible with democracy. If it were possible to grasp the absolute good, all means to attain it would be justified: violence, autocracy, dictatorship, tyranny. Democracy is compromise and presupposes value-relativism and ignorance of the substance of values.

Kelsen ends his beautiful and persuasive essay by retelling the story of Christ and Pontius Pilate according to the Gospel of St. John. When Jesus was brought before him, Pilate asked him: "Art thou the King of the Jews?" and Jesus answered: "Thou sayest that I am King. To this end I was born, and for this cause I came into this world, that I should bear witness unto the truth" (John 18:37). Pilate, a product of an old, tired and therefore skeptical civilization asked: "What is truth?" And because he does not know what truth is and because he—as a Roman—is accustomed to think democratically, he appealed to the people and arranged for a vote.

---

[7] *Ibid.*, p. 30.

[8] Hans Kelsen, *Vom Wesen und Wert der Demokratie* (Tübingen: Verlag J. C. B. Mohr [Paul Siebeck], 1920).

And this vote results in the crucifixion of Christ and the release of Barabbas who was a murderer.[9] Kelsen himself feels that this may rather be an argument against relativistic democracy; but he concludes that this would be a valid argument only if the holders of a political opinion are as certain of their truth as the son of God.

This is one of the most impressive formulations of the basic question of value-relativism and of the conflict between subjective and objective reason in political philosophy. Kelsen is right: no human being can be as sure of the truth and of the good as the son of God; but in spite of this uncertainty, human beings have to try to find the truth and to base their decisions on what for them is, at this historical moment, the truth and the good based on what they sincerely believe to be objective reason; otherwise they will release the murderer and condemn the son of God to death. There has to be a belief in the possibility of finding the true and the good and agreeing on it; otherwise society is open to chaos and anarchism. There would be no basis for the moral condemnation of such institutions as slavery and genocide. Everything that happens today in the public realm clearly indicates this. The present absence of belief in objective reason is an important source of our alienation and anomie, and of the rebellious restlessness in Western society.

The distinctions between objective and subjective, substantial and formal reason represent stages of intellectual history. The development went from a central world outlook with firmly believed values to value-relativism and value-pluralism. The medieval Thomists believed that their interpretation of the world and their value system was not only based on revelation, but arrived at by reason and had objective validity. The same is true of the philosophers of the Enlightenment. They secularized the religious world outlook; but they deduced their values from nature and reason, and thus created a new central world outlook. However, the idea that one can derive values from a central world outlook was gradually abandoned during the last hundred years in the West, and has given way to value-pluralism and value-relativism.

---

[9] *Ibid.*, p. 38. Translation mine.

A central world outlook, successful repression and values confirmed by reason form an interdependent network which gives the individual the necessary psychological and intellectual safety. The absence of this syndrome must lead to alienation and disintegration. This is what has happened in the West. To talk about the reduction and demotion of reason from encompassing to technical reason is another way of talking about this disintegration and alienation. Every society requires some degree of repression. This repression is not too burdensome—it may not even be experienced as repression—as long as it is justified by a world outlook and a central belief system, and if this belief system is experienced as reasonable and, therefore, as objectively valid. The dissection, demotion and reduction of reason is one special aspect of the process of disintegration which was and is both an intellectual and a psychological trend. Intellectually it consisted in the demotion and reduction of reason to technical reason and in the abandonment of morality as a valid category of life; psychologically, it consisted in the weakening of repression.[10]

In the light of this historical interpretation, the idea of value-neutrality in science assumes a different meaning. If one identifies science with knowledge in the broadest sense, such knowledge should be applicable to values (see above pp. 27 ff.). As we can see from the great civilizations—for example, the Greek polis and the high Middle Ages—cognitive rational systems can be alloyed with values, and reason can be used in pursuit of the good. Thus, it is not so that science, defined as encompassing, cognitive knowledge, must be value-neutral and cannot teach anything about the normative. But, during the last two hundred years in the West, the normative was eliminated from cognitive knowledge and the latter demoted to value-free, or rather value-empty science. Science thus became the pursuit of knowledge for practical technological application, a discipline which endeavors to predict and control the external world.

However, the normative is an essential aspect of human existence. If it is ignored and repressed it will return and manifest

---

[10] Compare Jürgen Habermas, *Technik und Wissenschaft als Ideologie* (Frankfurt am Main: Suhrkamp Verlag, 1968), p. 90.

itself in one form or another. Men have to believe in values which guide their actions. When people begin to believe that science is a value-free form of cognition and that all truth comes from science and only from science—then science has to hide its implicit value-judgments behind statements of fact. This, as we shall demonstrate, is the case in much of economic reasoning; in spite of its attempt to be "positive," economics has an implicitly normative content. This is true of a good deal of modern social theory and thought.[11] There, normative judgments hide behind factual statements because only the latter are supposed to be "scientific" and therefore true. This process had already started in the eighteenth century with the secularization of Christian beliefs. By grounding them in nature and reason rather than in divine revelation (and reason), the normative was translated into the factual, although, in the world outlook of the Enlightenment, normative and fiduciary elements (elements of faith) based on objective reason were still present. The situation of modern social science is then an ambiguous one; it postulates that it should be value-free and pretends to have fulfilled this postulate; however, because it claims to be the only source of truth and validity, it must and does unconsciously and implicitly include value-judgments. Normative judgments have been confined to the foster home of "science."

Some readers will undoubtedly cry out by now: But what about the contention that facts and values are different dimensions, that the "ought to" cannot be derived from what "is"? The answer I suggest is that such a distinction involves a repression of the normative, the ethical and the moral dimension. Men cannot live without values and they cannot embrace values without believing that they have validity. This is especially true of ultimate values which give meaning to life and meaning to death, of ideals for which men are ready to die. Without such ideals human existence is deprived of ends, goals and meanings, and exposed to alienation and to disintegration. This pragmatic approach should be sufficient to raise some doubts about the reasoning which leads to value-

---

[11] See Gunnar Myrdal, *The Political Element in the Development of Economic Theory* (Cambridge, Mass.: Harvard University Press, 1955), and *Value in Social Theory* (New York: Harper & Brothers, 1958).

relativity and separates values from reason. When values are inaccessible to reason, everything is permissible. There would be no basis on which one could condemn anything. No human being thinks, feels, acts and behaves that way; in one's daily life one continuously uses value-judgments based on norms to which one attributes objective validity. The idea that values are merely the result of nonrational factors is an intellectual aberration of modern civilization and a phenomenon of decay.

RATIONALISM AND IMPULSE CONTROL

Western alienation and repression led to the reduction of reason, the elimination of the normative and to impulse control. This latter aspect has been brought to light in the work of Max Weber. I do not propose to discuss all of his ideas on this subject but to direct attention to a few passages which express significantly the inner conflict of his time.

In relating the Protestant ethic to what he called the spirit of capitalism,[12] Max Weber was not concerned with either alienation or repression. Yet, it is not too farfetched to read into his image of the capitalistic spirit a pattern of gigantic repression and to see in the methodical, systematic, continuous pursuit of gain with avoidance of all enjoyment a way of life which is deeply in conflict with certain human inclinations. There is a definite similarity in the pattern of thought of Weber and Freud; although they approached the human situation from an entirely different vantage point, they both were concerned with impulse control and with the relation of self-restraint to social institutions.

According to Weber the spirit of capitalism involved intensive impulse- and self-control unknown in previous precapitalist economies. It required internal and external discipline. It imposed a moral obligation to postpone and sacrifice need satisfaction. It imposed a moral obligation to refrain from gratification as far as it is not necessary for keeping alive and fit. It was permeated by an anticonsumption orientation. It imposed the moral obligation of

---

[12] Max Weber, *The Protestant Ethic and the Spirit of Capitalism*, trans. by T. Parsons (New York: Charles Scribner's Sons, 1930).

continuous hard work in one's occupation, a moral obligation of "doing a good job." It required the renunciation of idleness, sloth, gossip, enjoyment of the senses, prodigality. It imposed the obligation to save, to refrain from luxurious and unnecessary consumption and expenditure. It was hostile even to relaxation, to friendship and close, human relations. Max Weber termed all this "worldly asceticism," by which he meant the impulse- and self-control required by industrial capitalism.

Worldly asceticism was a means toward the end of acquiring wealth, riches, possessions, money. "The summum bonum of this ethic is the earning of more and more money combined with the strict avoidance of all enjoyment." [13] It was an inner-directed orientation to use Riesman's term (*The Lonely Crowd*). The acquisition of wealth was the well-defined goal; economic rationality and impulse-control were the means to accomplish this goal. The goal was originally based on a religious belief in predestination and in economic success as proof of salvation. In the nineteenth century this religious belief was replaced by the conviction that economic success proved the individual's worth and superiority over the less successful ones who are failures in the competitive struggle, a conviction that has by no means been given up even today. The goal of acquisition and of economic success, whether for religious or other reasons, provided the rationalization and legitimation of all repression involved in worldly asceticism. This is a clear illustration of the principle previously discussed: repression has to be legitimized by a belief system which is rooted in a central world outlook in order to be tolerable and acceptable.

Worldly asceticism was exacerbated by its combination with rationalism (technical reason). Economic success was supposed to be pursued continuously, persistently, methodically, systematically. The ethos of early capitalism does not aim at acquisition as such. The "making of a fast buck" or the predatory, fraudulent, speculative making of profits is not in line with this ethos. What became institutionalized in the capitalist enterprise with profit- loss-

---

[13] *Ibid.,* p. 51.

and capital-accounting was preceded by an orientation in which the individual "acts like a firm and the individual conscience like the firm's auditor." [14]

Technical and economic rationalism was part of the system of impulse-control and repression of early capitalism. At first glance this may not be obvious because, in the course of the development of capitalism, impulse-control became separated from technical rationality, and economic rationalism was then combined with utilitarian hedonism see below pp. 71 ff.). The repressive effects of rationalism are, therefore, not as obvious as those of worldly asceticism. However, being inner-directed in a systematic, continuous, persistent way, and pursuing the goal of enrichment to the exclusion of other goals was, according to Max Weber, a new historical phenomenon. This new rationalism was so repressive that it was experienced as irrational from the precapitalist, and later from the utilitarian and hedonistic point of view.

Max Weber pointed out the repressive effects of economic rationalism at a time when economic thought, in neoclassical price theory, represented rational economic behavior as a *natural* mode of striving toward need satisfaction and built its entire interpretation of economic action on this premise. However, economic and bureaucratic rationalism is not a natural trait and involves a great deal of renunciation and self-control. Thus, economic rationalism is an important cause of repression and alienation in industrial society. Originally, worldly asceticism and rationalism formed an inseparable value syndrome. The Puritan was not simply supposed to be economically successful regardless of how it is accomplished. Calvinism eliminated "magic as a means of salvation," unifying life into a *methodical* system. "The moral conduct of the average man was thus deprived of its planless and unsystematic character and subject to a consistent method for conduct as a whole." [15] Here, the interdependence of asceticism and rationalism is obvious. "Irrational" impulses had to be eliminated. All impulses were considered as irrational which interfered with the suc-

---

[14] David Riesman, *The Lonely Crowd* (New Haven, Conn.: The Yale University Press, 1950).

[15] Max Weber, *Protestant Ethic*, pp. 117, 119.

cessful pursuit of wealth and riches, and with production for the market.

Methodical, rational self-control became an ideal in the free market system; this is what Max Weber called the "spirit of capitalism." He defined it as a *rational economic ethic*.[16] This definition contains the elements of rationality and normativity. The "spirit of capitalism" is an ethic, that is a normative, a value system. Its peculiar kind of systematic, methodical, repressive pursuit of wealth is considered as a moral obligation. It was a repressive ethic because it imposed the restrictive rules of rational action and because it "is, above all, completely devoid of any eudaemonistic, not to say hedonistic admixture." Economic, technical rationality and repression of enjoyment were originally inseparable.

This interdependence of repression and rationality in the Puritan-Calvinist capitalist value complex is clearly stated by Bendix: [17]

The Calvinist "could not hope to atone for hours of weakness or thoughtlessness by increased good will at other times . . . There was no place for the very human Catholic cycle of sin, repentance, atonement, release, followed by renewed sin . . . The moral conduct of the average man was thus deprived of its *planless* and *unsystematic* character . . . Only a life guided by *constant thought* could achieve conquest over a state of nature. It was this rationalization which gave the reformed faith its peculiar ascetic tendency . . ." [18]

The symbiosis of rationality with the repression of human propensities toward relaxation, release, laziness, sin and planlessness—that is, its combination of rationality with impulse-control —could not be expressed in a clearer fashion. Even a denial of satisfaction with the creative experience in work was inherent in this value system because "drudgery itself was a means of attain-

---

[16] Max Weber, *General Economic History*, trans. by F. H. Knight (Glencoe, Ill.: The Free Press, 1927, 1950), chap. XXX, p. 354; also *Gesammelte Aufsätze zur Wissenschaftslehre* (Tübingen: Verlag J. C. B. Mohr [Paul Siebeck], 1922), p. 30.
[17] Reinhard Bendix, *Max Weber* (Garden City, N.Y.: Doubleday Anchor Books, 1962), p. 60, italics mine.
[18] Max Weber, *Protestant Ethic*, pp. 117–18.

ing the certainty of grace." [19] These quotations refer to the Protestant-Calvinist-Puritan syndrome but their congruity with and applicability to the early capitalist value system is obvious.

The present rebellion against the discipline of modern life proves the point. The beatniks, hippies, yippies and militants reject both industrial discipline and rationality. In doing so they try to shake off the shackles of a century-old repression whose existence they prove by their rebellion. One does not have to approve of this rebellion in order to understand it in terms of a dialectical process in which the repressed provides the dynamics for rebellion. This rebellion and emergence of the repressed, if unchecked, may destroy the basis of industrial society. What is needed is a balance between repressive rationalism and discipline on the one hand, and outlets for the repressed factors and forces on the other hand. In terms of Herbert Marcuse (*Eros and Civilization*) the "surplus repression" implied in industrial rationalism and impulse-control has to be eliminated to accomplish this balance.

In this discussion one has to be on guard against using such terms as rationality and irrationality as if their meaning were invariable; they are relative concepts. What is rational from one point of view can be irrational from another one.

Modern Western culture of which capitalism is a part, developed as an antithesis to the religious, magical and traditionalist attitudes of the medieval period. From the precapitalist point of view the new value-attitude syndrome of the spirit of capitalism did not "make sense"; worldly asceticism and its rational discipline were experienced as "irrational." Considered in the light of the Protestant, Puritan spirit of capitalism, however, the old attitude was its antithesis and therefore "irrational." If modern society is called a "rational" society, the old magic, traditionalist, value-attitude system can be called "irrational." The new value system combined impulse repression with technical, economic means-end rationality. This alliance between impulse-control, rationalism and a belief system which supported these repressions was undermined by the very rationalism which it supported. Under the impact of

---

[19] Bendix, *loc cit.*, p. 64.

critical reasoning, religious beliefs disintegrated from the eighteenth century onward. However, they were replaced by a secular belief system in the form of social Darwinism. Both systems provided the acquisitive, self-controlled, achievement-oriented, inner-directed individual not only with a good conscience but attributed to his economic success the dignity of a special virtue. It enabled him to feel superior to his less successful fellowmen either because he believed that he was among the chosen or because he considered himself to be more fit than others in the fight for survival. However, under the impact of rationalism, any kind of repression became untenable. Technical reason did not support impulse-control in the service of the never-ending pursuit of wealth without satisfaction or enjoyment. Rationalism led to the recognition that impulse-control is "irrational" from the point of view of satisfaction and of the pleasure principle. This destruction of the basis for impulse-control was accelerated by the growing abundance in industrial capitalism which made the "avoidance of all enjoyment" appear as entirely irrational. The very success of capitalism in increasing material productivity and in raising standards of living undermined worldly asceticism with its repressive features of self-control and denial of enjoyment. With Protestant, Calvinist, Puritan and similar beliefs abandoned, the very rock on which worldly asceticism rested was gone; the growing abundance of material goods presented too much of a temptation and made "the avoidance of enjoyment" well-nigh impossible. Enjoyment and pleasure became accepted goals of economic conduct. This was reflected in classical and neoclassical economics through the adoption of utilitarianism and of the pleasure principle. Economic action was supposed to be motivated by the striving for happiness, utility and maximum satisfaction of needs, wants, desires and tastes.

The tradition of thrift and anticonsumption asceticism, however, was still alive. Thus, a conflict arose between economic rationalism founded on ascetic restraints on the one hand, and the later economic rationalism based on the utilitarian pleasure principle on the other hand. If pleasure and the satisfaction of subjective desires are ultimate goals, what forces are left which would compel the individual to act like an economically rational being in capitalist society is supposed to act? What could then compel rational, deliberate, planned, self-controlled action, hard work, saving and investing, and acquiring in a methodical systematic fashion? What would prevent man from being erratic, spontaneous, expressive, playful, living out feelings and emotions, being, at times, chaotic, anarchic and even destructive? The dialectical conflict between subjective pleasures and disciplined, rational behavior became a crucial problem of Western society, capitalist and communist alike. On the one hand, any restriction of the subjective pleasure principle as the ultimate regulator of human action seems to be incompatible with the economistic, physiological, consumerist, pleasure-principled individualism of today's Western society. On the other hand, industrial production and organization require rational discipline.

Today, we are living in a period in which the adoration of the subjective pleasure principle changes our society and its value-attitudes from within. This situation creates alienation: industrial, technological, organizational and scientific rationalism still represses the drive for pleasure. However, resistance against inner, chaotic, anarchic pleasure drives has become weaker. If what today is called the "counterculture" should become, with help from the mass media, the dominant life-style, it could make rational discipline in technology and business impossible.

This conflict is not a new one. For a century, technical rationalism undermined *all* belief systems which could have supported any kind of repression, even the one inherent in social, technical, organizational, bureaucratic rationalism itself. The present-day affluent economy deprived any repression inherent in this rational society of a legitimizing principle; the surfeit of goods reduces the pleasure derived from more goods and puts in doubt the belief that economic activity has anything to do with need satisfaction.[20]

The final outcome of this development is that "science and technology themselves become ideologies." Science and technology with their inherent repressive rationalism become ends,

[20] See J. K. Galbraith, *The Affluent Society* (Boston: Houghton Mifflin Company, 1958), and below pp. 160 ff.

belief systems and rationalizations supporting the status quo and the power of the elite which rests on the application of this rationalism. However, one should not even call science and technology ideologies or rationalizations because, being value-empty means, they are not able to support, legitimize, rationalize, justify their own existence. This is the situation we find ourselves in now. The main institutions and activities of Western society, technologically oriented science, technology and the economy exist for their own sake. They have no justification in any superordinated, all-embracing value system. Their only *raison d'être* is their own self-perpetuation. The main reason why people tolerate them is that their individual existence is enmeshed in these institutions and their livelihood and security depend on them. It is hardly surprising that under these conditions the more sensitive groups of modern youth feel deeply anomic, frustrated and alienated and that they try to escape the repression of a system which has lost all basis in any faith, belief, central world outlook or value system.

THE PATTERN OF ALIENATION
IN WESTERN SOCIAL THOUGHT

When technical, instrumental, subjective formalized reason and reasoning destroy the central belief system which supports repression, the individual, deprived of rationalization of his value system, begins to experience repression as an intolerable burden. The period of Western history when the central world outlook and its value system began to disintegrate was the precise period when the actual phenomenon of repression was discovered. At the same time an ideal was projected into the past and into the future, while present values, beliefs and institutions with their repressions were condemned.

This process started long before Freud. Western social thought since the eighteenth century has developed what has been called a model of alienation.[21] This model assumes that there is

---

21 Jakobus Wössner, *Sozialnatur und Sozialstruktur* (Berlin: Dunker & Humblot, 1965), pp. 17 ff., especially pp. 22 ff. on which the following section on Rousseau is based.

homo ante—man before he is socialized, when he is a design, a potentiality; and there is *homo post*, man after socialization, when he becomes alienated and reduced to a part of his total potentialities through social restrictions. Wössner considers this process of socialization as a process of becoming human, and, at the same time, as a process of becoming alienated. Through socialization *homo ante*, man before society, becomes *homo post*, man who is alienated from his previous essence.[22] This was and is the main theme of Western social thought since the eighteenth century. Because the central world outlook and value system which supported repression have been weakened and finally destroyed, Western man becomes conscious of alienation.

For Rousseau *homo ante* is man in his natural state before he becomes a member of society. In this state he is free and independent; he does what he wants, his will is free and only restricted by his needs. In this natural state man is happy and in harmony with his environment.[23] The resistance of nature to the satisfaction of needs leads to cooperation in the form of a division of labor and to the development of political institutions. In order to protect themselves against scarcity and other dangers, individuals band together in society. Society, however, brings about law, domination and inequality. It is the fall from original innocence, the beginning of alienation.

This scheme established the pattern of social thought for two centuries to come. It played a role in the thought of Marx and it is the pattern which underlies Freudian thought. "Homme de la nature" (*homo ante*) becomes "homme policé" (*homo post*). The alienation, the fall from innocence and grace, from freedom and happiness, is brought about by society, culture, civilization—by the power of man over man, domination and division of labor.[24]

Wössner interprets Rousseau's alienation model as a hidden intellectual weapon, a critical "utopia." Behind the general critique of society as an alienating factor lurks the critique of French society, of the *ancien régime;* it was part of the intellectual prepara-

---

22 *Ibid.*, p. 19.
23 *Ibid.*, pp. 22 ff.
24 *Ibid.*, p. 24.

tion for the French Revolution. This applies generally to the social alienation scheme; whenever an uncorrupted *homo ante* is juxtaposed to a socially corrupted and alienated *homo post*, a conscious or unconscious critique of existing society is implied. This critique is a symptom of the disintegration of the central world outlook and value system. When it crumbles, a scheme emerges in which *homo ante* is interpreted as good and society as "bad." At the same time, the new ideal which is supposed to overcome the dichotomy of "good" presocialized and "bad" socialized man is projected into the future: a temporal utopia in which the antinomy with its alienation is dissolved in a new union of opposites.

There is a distinction between technical and critical reason. *Critical reason* is released when the central world outlook and the existing value system lose their hold over the minds of people. Traditional cognitive and normative patterns are dissolving and critical reason is liberated. This has to be distinguished from *technical reason* which is confined to means, is subjectivized, formalized and not utopian: it cannot, like critical reason, provide a new value system and a new world outlook. The borderline between the two types of reason is fluid. Critical reason became technical only in the nineteenth century when value-relativism, formalization and subjectivization were setting in. In the eighteenth century there were still objective elements in critical reason which were retained in spite of the secularization of values. It became technical when reason lost all substantive content and its claim toward objective validity.

Rousseau, however, had not yet reached the stage of technical, formalized value-relativistic reasoning. He tried to replace the world outlook and the value system of the French monarchy with a democratic political philosophy based on the concepts of the social contract and the general will.[25] He tried to eliminate the conflict between *ex ante* freedom and *ex post* unfreedom. For this purpose he reinterpreted freedom *ex ante* as submission to the laws of *nature;* correspondingly he then reinterpreted the alienated state of socialized man as *social* freedom, defined as submission to the

---

[25] *Ibid.,* pp. 26 ff.

laws of society, that is to the general will. Thus, social alienation is negated by social community in which individual wills merge into the harmony of superindividual consensus. Wössner sees here a first glimpse of the distinction between alienating society and unifying community. This amalgamation of individuals into a community requires an elite of enlightened persons (like Plato's philosopher-kings) to educate the masses, to lead them toward an understanding of the common good, and to direct the common will.

The pattern of modern social thought was set by Rousseau: the ideal state, before socialization of the individual; the fall after socialization and alienation from the natural human essence which implies a critique of existing institutions and values; and finally, a new construct which justifies and legitimizes socialization again by redefining individual liberty as social freedom through the formation of a general will under the guidance of an elite. The new construct is destined to negate the dialectical antinomy of unalienated man and alienated socialized man. It is used in democratic political theory and in the ideas of consumers' sovereignty and the optimum allocation of resources through the free market (see below pp. 160 ff.).

3

The Struggle Between the Normative and the Value-Relativistic Approach in Economic Thought

Economic thought, as used here, refers to the philosophical, ethical, moral and normative ideas implicit in economic reasoning. The value system which underlies economic thought can be distilled from the writings of economists and economic philosophers. Attention has to be paid not to the models and mathematical techniques but to what modern economics neglects: the implicit presuppositions and tacit assumptions of economic thought about human nature, human goals, aspirations, values, impulses and drives and the philosophical outlook implied in economic reasoning. The system of philosophy and values implied and somewhat hidden in economic thought reflects the spirit of the times, or, at least, the spirit of a large subculture of the historical period in which these ideas were developed. The ideas which took hold in the history of economic thought influenced the opinions and actions of businessmen and politicians, and reflect a supraindividual social and cultural situation. These ideas deal with the conflicts, antinomies, alienations and repressions I have already discussed. They try to reconcile these conflicts and bring about a unified world outlook.

Changes in economic value-attitudes correlate with the development from a laissez-faire, free market system to a mixed economy involving governmental and corporate market power. The free market system and the laissez-faire philosophy were, at first, combined with an ethos of impulse control and rational discipline oriented toward hard work in production and thrift for the purpose of capital formation. This stage is represented by classical economics which contained the remnants of a central belief and of a substantive value system.

Utilitarian hedonism and neoclassical economics which followed still retained some of these elements; but they moved toward an elimination of normative concepts and led finally to a model of the free market system based on ethical relativism. The economic system was assumed to satisfy the full uncontrolled gratification of subjective desires and impulses.

These schools of economic thought interpreted the economy as an autonomous self-regulating cybernetic system where the feedback of consumer demand regulated the flow of resources and production. But the growth in market power by corporate and public managers has seemed to interfere with autonomous self-regulation by impersonal market forces. Questions have arisen: whom do managers represent, to whom are they responsible and, finally, what are the goals of economic activity? So far discussions of these questions remain inconclusive: on the one hand, they lead to an attempt to reintroduce moral values into economics; on the other hand, they treat technical innovation and economic growth as ends in themselves.

I trace these developments in the following three chapters.

CLASSICAL ECONOMICS

Political economy became an autonomous discipline in the eighteenth century and in the early nineteenth century. Classical economists, especially Adam Smith, replaced the religious "Protestant" foundation of the economic ethos by a naturalistic philosophy based on the ideas of Locke, the Scottish school of philosophy and the Enlightenment. In line with the intellectual tendency of this period, God was replaced by nature, and religion by the science of nature; but this system of thought did not lack a basis in objective reason. The restraints and repressions required by the market economy were grounded in a natural philosophy which interpreted its values and directives as rooted in the nature of man and society and as being part of the structure of the universe, thereby providing ideological roots and moral justification.

The main problems of early capitalism were: to increase the production of physical goods through technological improvements and to procure a sufficient surplus of capital to put new inventions into effect. Capital accumulation was required to increase productive equipment, and thereby the volume of production in order to meet the needs of a rising population and the expectations of rising standards of living. This increase in productive capacity and productivity required impulse control: for industrial discipline in factory production, for hard systematic work, saving and thrift; and it required an acquisitive orientation leading to the production of ever more durable goods. This economic style of life was new. Its Puritan, religious foundation was on the wane. Adam Smith justified and legitimized the new economic life-style by the concepts of individual economic self-interest, by the natural harmony of interests and by the labor theory of value. All these ideas represent a secularization of the Puritan ethos, a theoretical legitimization of the impulse controls and rational discipline required in capitalism.

The classical economists represent the individual as striving naturally for the accumulation of money and riches as ends in themselves; he is supposed to work industriously for economic success, producing more and more, competing with others, forgoing the pleasure of luxurious consumption, and accumulating surplus in the form of capital. The individual is assumed to exert himself continuously to increase the capital at his disposal. Classical economics maintained that acquisition is an innate natural human trait. The *Wealth of Nations* abounds with statements to prove this point. "The desire of bettering our condition comes with us from

the womb and never leaves us until we go to the grave." [1] Equally
clear is the pronouncement that "every individual is continuously
exerting himself to find out the most advantageous employment for
whatever capital he can command." [2] The implicit intention of
such statements is to make unlimited acquisition respectable and
acceptable by interpreting it as rooted in human nature and thereby
justifying it. In a society with a secularized, nonreligious belief
system based on empiricism, naturalism and rationalism, only
nature interpreted by "science" can morally justify action and behavior. By calling something a natural propensity and an innate inclination such justification is implied. Although the acquisition of
more and more, the goal of economic growth, becomes meaningless
in an affluent society (see chap. 6), in early capitalism this ideal
was not meaningless because of the situation of relative scarcity of
means of production and a population rising in both numbers and
expectations. However, Adam Smith and the classical school of
economics certainly erred in interpreting the acquisitive attitude
as a natural human inclination. Such an interpretation represents
the elevation of a culture-bound historical orientation to a universal
principle. It is even doubtful whether there is an innate drive
toward "bettering one's situation." But even if this were granted
for the sake of argument, one has to admit that what human beings
consider as "bettering themselves" could be radically different from
the acquisitive attitude. It may be freedom *from* the work discipline, the possibility to loaf, to have leisure, to contemplate, to do
nothing, combined with a target income which would ensure the
necessities of life and not more and more so-called comforts, frills
and consumption "kicks."

Adam Smith had to interpret the term self-interest in a narrowly circumscribed way: to mean the acquisition of more and
more money, riches and possessions, and nothing else. The term
self-interest is thus restricted in two ways. First it is reduced to
economic interests; then economic self-interest is defined as the

---

[1] Adam Smith, *An Inquiry into the Nature and Causes of the Wealth of
Nations* (New York: Random House, Modern Library, 1937), p. 324.
[2] *Ibid.*, p. 421.

striving for more and more money and purchasing power. This restrictive definition of self-interest was necessary to justify economic egoism and greed from a social point of view. This was accomplished by his theory of the natural harmony of individual and social interests.[3] Adam Smith arrived at this doctrine by defining individual and social interest in the same way: as increase in production. The individual accomplishes an increase in wealth by producing more goods for exchange on the market; in this way he promotes the public interest by adding to the sum of goods produced. By producing more he increases his own wealth and, simultaneously, the wealth of the nation.

"As every individual . . . endeavors as much as he can to employ his capital in the support of domestic industry, and so to direct that industry that its produce may be of the greatest value; every individual necessarily labors to render the annual revenue of society as great as he can . . . he intends his own security . . . only his own gain . . . and he is in this, as in many other cases, led by an invisible hand, to promote an end which was no part of his intention.[4]

This famous passage (containing Adam Smith's only reference to the invisible hand) shows clearly how, by defining social and individual interest in the same way, namely as increases in production, Adam Smith must arrive at his doctrine of harmony. The individual pursues his own gain by producing more; society (implicitly defined atomistically, as the sum total of individuals) has the same goal, the increase in the total produce.

A historically relative situation is elevated to an absolute principle in order to justify its goals. If, indeed, the production of more and more goods regardless of what these goods are and regardless of their distribution is in the common interest, individual acquisitiveness leading to an increase in individual production will promote the common good, and justify the egotistic greed which allegedly motivates economic action. If individuals strive for the accumulation of money and capital, the result will be beneficial for

---

[3] E. Halévy, *The Growth of Philosophic Radicalism* (New York: Augustus M. Kelley, 1949).
[4] *Ibid.*, p. 423.

society as a whole as if an "invisible hand" would guide their steps in this direction. The moral problem of early capitalism consisted of convincing people that their self-interest lay in the pursuit of economic gain, and not in noneconomic goals as was believed in previous periods; that is why economic thought had to stress the naturalness and beneficiality of this type of conduct. Also, Adam Smith's idea of the natural harmony of interests solved the problem as to how an economic order can rise if individuals are given complete economic liberty, the basic problem of any individualistic social philosophy. If it can be asserted that: (1) individual economic self-interest consists in monetary gain; (2) monetary gain can be accomplished by the individual producing and then selling an increased amount of products; (3) the public interest consists in increasing the total volume of goods sold on the market—then it could be maintained that private and public economic interests are not in conflict but in harmony with each other. These ideas and definitions of Adam Smith were the origin of the ideal of economic growth which will occupy us later (chap. 6).

Another central idea of this intellectual structure is the concept of labor as the basis of value. The labor theory of value served as a focus for the legal, economic, ethical, technological and scientific orientations of the period. Already, John Locke had justified private property as the product of the physical labor of an individual. The new economic morality elevated labor and work to the dignity of a life goal. By explaining that relative prices conformed to relative efforts (quantities of labor), an ethical basis was provided for the exchange economy. At the same time, labor was the main factor of production in a period when the use of machinery and steam power was in its infancy; production appeared as a process in which labor applied to land and raw materials created the produce. This conception conformed to the style of thought of physics and mechanics; labor represented a force or energy, setting matter into motion. By making labor the "foundation, cause, and measure" of economic value, the classical economists thus chose a symbol which, with one stroke, combined and unified the major preoccupations of their time. Exchange relations and market prices appeared to be in harmony with and determined by the same cause as phenomena in the rest of the social and natural universe. The philosophical essence of the labor theory of value is that the value of a commodity is determined by the amount of labor which was used in its production. It is not necessary to enter here into a discussion of all of the problems connected with this theory, for example, whether it relates only to relative prices or intends to find an absolute yardstick for a value, and how labor of different quality can be reduced to a common quantitative denominator. What matters here is the ethical and psychological basis of this value theory. It is the feeling that economic reward should be commensurate with effort, that differences in reward should correspond to differences in merit—an experience which seems deeply rooted in industrial capitalism; it is the same idea which underlies the union slogan: equal pay for equal work; which also could be formulated as: more pay for more work. Interpreted in this fashion, *the labor theory of value is a translation of the Puritan work ethic into the language of classical economics.* The Puritan believed that hard work was pleasing to God and that if he accomplished economic success through hard work he proved that he was chosen and blessed by the Lord. Thus, hard work is rewarded in consonance with effort. The same idea is implied in the labor theory of value. The greater the work effort the greater the value and market price of the product and the greater the amount of purchasing power acquired by the sale of this product. Greater effort thus brings with it a higher financial reward. This psychological basic of the labor theory is still alive in the egalitarian critique of excessively high income, for example, of top executives, and entertainers. The critique is based on the feeling: is there such a difference between my effort and the effort put in by these persons that would justify the enormous difference in incomes? In spite of our prevalent explanation of prices and incomes in terms of the relation between their supply and the demand for them, this feeling, underlying the labor theory of value, still persists.

Even the marginal productivity theory which is generally accepted today shows traces of this approach. The marginal productivity theory maintains that in a free market the income of a worker is determined by his marginal contribution to the economy.

The ditchdigger contributes little (mainly because there are so many ditchdiggers, and they are unskilled workers); the surgeon receives a high income because he contributes much(mainly because there are relatively few surgeons). This theory is sometimes used to justify the existing income distribution; but the financial and social obstacles to becoming a surgeon and the impossibility for many workers to rise above the rank of the unskilled are overlooked. The Marxist slogan: "from everybody according to his productive contribution, to everybody according to his needs," is rejected. This rejection is based on the same idea as the labor theory of value; namely, that reward should be commensurate with effort under the assumption that higher productive contribution requires greater effort. The surgeon puts in quantitively and qualitatively more effort than the ditchdigger. His contribution is greater and therefore his reward higher. Although one's productive contribution depends on the scarcity of the service rendered and not merely on individual merit, there is an underlying conviction that the service is scarce because it requires exceptional talent, training and skill which is acquired through greater effort.

The work and success ethic of Puritan asceticism with its ethos of thrift, saving and accumulation of capital also found its counterpart in Adam Smith's praise of parsimony and his condemnation of prodigality. The entire book II, chapter III, of his *Wealth of Nations* is a panegyric on saving and a condemnation of spending. It is based on his distinction between productive and unproductive labor which is clearly a value judgment in favor of productive labor. Productive labor is "good" because it leads to the production of durable goods which can be used in further employment and production and yield a profit. Productive labor "realizes itself in a . . . vendible commodity which lasts for some time at least after that labor is past . . . It is . . . a certain quantity of labor stocked and stored up to be employed . . ." [5] That saving and production of durables which lead to capital formation are praised not as merely utilitarian devices but as reflections of an ethos can be seen from this passage:

---

[5] *Wealth of Nations*, p. 314.

"Wherever capital predominates, *industry* prevails; wherever revenue, *idleness* . . . Capitals are increased by parsimony, and diminished by prodigality and *misconduct*. Parsimony . . . is the immediate cause of the increase in capital . . . That portion of his revenue that a rich man annually spends is in most cases consumed by idle guests and menial servants who leave nothing behind in return for their consumption. That portion which he annually saves is consumed . . . by a different set of people, by laborers, manufacturers, and artificers who reproduce with a profit the value of their annual consumption . . . what a frugal man annually saves . . . affords maintenance to an additional number of productive hands . . . the perpetual allotment of this fund . . . is guarded . . . by *a very powerful principle the plain and evident interest of every individual* to whom a share of it shall ever belong." [6]

To Adam Smith, saving, parsimony, thrift, capital formation and employment are all positive values. He condemns the aristocrats and their luxury spending and "the most frivolous professions: churchmen, lawyers, physicians and men of letters of all kinds: players, buffoons, musicians, opera singers, opera dancers, etc." because their labor produces nothing which could afterward purchase or procure an equal quantity of labor.[7] And he interprets saving as an innate instinct. "But the principle which prompts us to save is *the desire of bettering our condition,* a desire which, though generally calm and dispassionate, comes with us from the womb, and never leaves us until we go to the grave." [8] It is all here, the entire syndrome of worldly asceticism; thrift and acquisition are ultimate ends, not interpreted as ordained by God but as instilled into us by nature. Adam Smith, in a naturalistic and seemingly empiricist philosophy, adopts the same system of value attitudes that Max Weber traces back to the Puritan ethic. The content is the same, only the interpretation as to its origin differs.

Like Rousseau, Adam Smith developed a dialectical historical scheme. In what he calls the early and rude state, that is in an economy where there is no appropriation of land and no capital

[6] *Ibid.,* pp. 321–22, italics mine.
[7] *Ibid.,* p. 315.
[8] *Ibid.,* p. 324.

accumulation (before capitalism), values and prices, that is rewards for economic activity, conform to effort. Goods in whose production more labor time has been used (more effort has been expended) will command higher prices; thus their producers will receive higher rewards. In this rude state there is no wage labor. Every producer—man *ex ante*—is an independent entrepreneur and receives the full price for which his product sells on the market; the harder he works the more he receives in exchange. Thus, this primordial early and rude state is implicitly an ideal one, corresponding to the Christian paradise. After appropriation of land and accumulation of capital in the hands of capitalists has taken place, the wage system emerges. Now, the price for which goods sell on the market has to be distributed to the laborer as wage, to the landlord who owns the land in the form of rent, and to the capitalist who owns the means of production (be they machines, or simply the food and materials which keep the workers alive during the period of production) in the form of profit (interest). This is the theory of natural price which Adam Smith developed in addition to his labor theory of value. The two theories reflect two different societies: the labor theory of value applies to the precapitalist economy where the producers (independent owners and enterprisers) are supposed to receive the full value of their product. The natural price theory applies in a capitalist economy with a profit and wage system where the exchange value of the product is distributed among the three classes, laborers, landlords and entrepreneurs in the form of wages, rents and profits. Here, the "producer" (the laborer)—man *ex post*—no longer receives the full value of his product. Adam Smith thus develops a prelapsarian and a postlapsarian theory of value and price, the "Fall" ("lapsus") being represented, as in Marx, by the emergence of private ownership of land and the means of production by persons who are not also workers and producers. Thus, the justification and the legitimation of prices in a free market economy as undertaken by Adam Smith suffered from its very outset from an ambivalence and a dialectical conflict which was later exploited by Marx. In the *Psychology of Economics* I analyze the tortuous way in which Ricardo tried to eliminate this conflict (see part III). He did not succeed and he had to admit in the end that at least capital and profits influence changes in relative prices; thus, the pure labor theory of value was untenable. This, however, meant failure in the attempt to justify the price system on ethical grounds. For the classical economists such a justification could rest only on the idea that differences in prices are caused by differences in the amount of labor used in the production of goods. The ethical justification of prices rested on the idea that economic rewards (prices and wages) are commensurate to effort and merit. Habermas formulates this as follows: as soon as an economy produces a surplus product over and above what is necessary for sheer survival, it has to develop a principle for distributing this surplus *unequally but legitimately*.[9] This is what the classical economists tried. Their attempt was beset with logical and psychological difficulties; however, for almost a century, their ideas served as justification for the price system until the time was ripe for Marx to uncover the inner contradictions and turn their reasoning around: The labor theory of value does not justify the existing price system as the classics thought; it reveals the exploitation of the worker through the appropriation of the surplus value by the capitalist in the form of profits. This is the form in which the critical reasoning of Marx translated the idea of alienation into economic language: the worker is alienated from his product; a part of it is taken away and appropriated by the capitalist.

MARX

Although Marx derived his dialectical scheme from Hegel, Adam Smith prepared the way for its application to economics by his distinction between the "early and rude" state without private ownership of the means of production and without a wage system, and the "advanced" state *with* those institutions.

The Marxist philosophy of history distinguishes an idealized state set against the "Fall," and a predicted synthesis on a higher social level. History begins, according to Engels, with a phase of

9 Jürgen Habermas, *Technik und Wissenschaft als Ideologie* (Frankfurt am Main: Suhrkamp Verlag, 1968), p. 66.

communism (Urkommunismus); the *ex post* phase is represented by the introduction of private property with class distinctions; the synthesis is the classless society in which private property, class distinctions and alienation are eliminated.

In his early writings Marx saw the cause of alienation in the division of labor and in specialization; they endangered the wholeness of man, and prevented man from realizing all his potentialities. He states that: ". . . in the communist society nobody has a narrowly circumscribed circle of activities but everybody can train himself in any branch of activity, and only society regulates general production, and makes possible for me to do this today and that tomorrow, to hunt in the morning, to fish in the afternoon, to raise cattle in the evening, to be a critic after dinner, just as I feel at the moment; without ever being hunter, fisherman, herdsman, or critic." [10] The utopian naïveté of these lines is astounding but less important than the fact that Marx, at a time when the industrial revolution on the Continent was in its infancy, set the tone for a critique which is still applicable today.

In this quotation the pattern of alienation can clearly be discerned: the goal of human life and existence is the actualization of the *whole* personality, the realization of all potentialities. This implies that there is a total personality with more potentialities than can be realized in industrial society. Like Hegel, Marx sees in allround creativity the main instrument of total self-actualization. In a way this is an industrial version of the all-round Renaissance man.

Hegel was concerned with the relation between subject and object, between the idea and its realization. He saw in labor and work the creative process in which the idea, reason and the spirit became incarnated in society and the state. Accordingly, to the young Marx, still under the influence of Hegel, labor and work are self-fulfillment; but not work within the capitalist order, because this kind of work is one-sided, fragmented, segmentalized, and represses human potentialities. For the younger Marx the division of labor is *the* repressive institution.

Marx interpreted economic activity in physiological terms.

[10] Karl Marx, *Die Deutsche Ideologie, Marx-Engels Gesamtausgabe* (MEGA), (Moskau-Leningrad, 1933), vol. V, p. 22, translation mine.

This is especially true of his concept of labor. The best formulation of what Marx meant by labor can be found in a work by a noneconomist, Hannah Arendt, in her book *The Human Condition*, "Labor is the activity which corresponds to the biological process of the human body, whose spontaneous growth, metabolism, and eventual decay are bound to the vital necessities produced and fed into the life process by labor. The human condition of labor is life itself." [11] For the young Marx labor was the essential human process by which man produces and thereby separates himself from an object. In consuming the objects man himself has created, he negates this separation and reunites subject and object.[12] Here, the Hegelian split between subject and object and the striving for union is translated into the economic language of production and consumption, and is understood as a physiological process of metabolism creating and supporting life itself by consuming whatever is produced. This process is disturbed when production is not fully "negated" by consumption. This disturbance is caused by capital and the capitalist who retains part of the product for capital accumulation and his own enrichment. The unequal distribution of the results of production—poverty caused by exploitation—disturbs the metabolic circle. But before there was private property, there had been freedom, that is, personal disposition of the product of labor through consumption: "The producers know what becomes of the product; they consume it, it does not leave their hands." [13] Before private property, the individual can freely dispose of and consume his product. Private property and the division of labor destroy this freedom and thereby cause alienation. Finally, in the classless society the collective ownership of the means of production leads to the negation of alienation: man is again reunited with the products of his labor.

What matters here is the basic scheme of alienation, not the

---

[11] Hannah Arendt, *The Human Condition* (Garden City, N.Y.: Doubleday Anchor Books, 1959). Arendt distinguishes labor from work which "corresponds to the unnaturalness of human existence . . . and provides an artificial world of things . . . which outlasts and transcends life." *Ibid.* Marx does not sharply distinguish between labor and work. See Arendt, part III.

[12] Marx, MEGA, vol. III, p. 156, vol. V, pp. 17 ff. Wössner, *loc. cit.*, pp. 44 ff.

[13] *Marx*, MEGA, vol. III, p. 124.

substance of these ideas. The earlier stage without alienation, the later stage with alienation, and the restoration of a nonalienated state on a higher plane of development are present in both Rousseau and in the ideas of the young and older Marx. The *ex ante* and the *ex post* scheme also underlies Adam Smith's distinction between the "early and rude state" and the "advanced society"; in the latter the worker has to share the total product with the landlord and the capitalist. This is what Marx considered as "expropriation." In his earlier writings and under the influence of Hegel, Marx interpreted this expropriation in a less economistic and more psychological way, as depriving the worker of his creativity, something like the repression of Veblen's instinct of workmanship.[14] In the *Capital* and in his later writings, this idea is, under the influence of the classical economists, reduced to the loss of a part of the price. This is derived from Adam Smith's concept of the natural price. The payment of rent and profit was a consequence of private property. Marx considered this private property and the rent and interest paid to its holders as exploitation of the worker, who should receive the entire price. While in the earlier writings alienation is attributed to the division of labor and the separation of the worker from his product, in the later writings alienation becomes exploitation; the worker is deprived of part of the price of the product. However, the basic pattern of alienation and repression is the same whether expressed in Hegelian terms or in the language of classical economics; the whole is reduced to one of its parts; the ensuing alienation, repression, deprivation and segmentalization are identified.

This is also the meaning of the tripartite scheme of Rousseau: the total freedom of the noble savage, the natural man before socialization, permitted realization of the total personality. The emergence of society restricted this freedom by reducing the total personality to one of his parts. Recognition of the alienating effects of the social system resulted from a disintegration of belief in the validity of the value system on which the restrictive society was based and by which its values were justified. The restriction of man

---

[14] Karl Loewith, "Max Weber and Karl Marx," in *Gesammelte Abhandlungen* (Stuttgart: Verlag W. Kohlhammer, 1960), pp. 1 ff.

to a part of his totality, his enclosure into a specific partial mold was and is a ubiquitous phenomenon; but men become aware of it and use this awareness for critical and revolutionary purposes only when the supporting belief system becomes unbelievable and untenable. Then, alienation and repression are recognized as such, whereas before they were hidden by the world outlook and the value system. When critical reason undermines this value system, alienation and repression emerge into the light of consciousness. In the case of Rousseau it was belief in the legitimacy of the absolute rule of king and court that disintegrated. In the case of Marx, belief in the beneficial nature of the free competitive market system and wage system had disintegrated. Therefore, Rousseau saw his society as repressive and Marx interpreted the capitalist economy as alienating and exploitative. In both cases, intellectual doubts about the central belief system which supported the existing institutions—the ancient regime and the competitive market economy based on private ownership—created the resulting awareness of repression, alienation and exploitation.

It should be noticed that the approach of the *early* writings of Marx must by necessity lead to a critique of *industrial* society whether it is capitalist, socialist or communist. Socialism and communism are said to eliminate the expropriation of the worker and reunite him with his product. It is debatable whether this is really accomplished by the nationalization of factories and of profit, and by governmental regulation of prices and production as it exists in Soviet Russia. Socialization and nationalization, however, do not remove the alienation caused by the division of labor, which persists in socialist and communist economies. The division of labor and its concomitant specialization and fragmentation of life are a consequence of modern technology and production organization, and of the complexity of modern mass society. It cannot be eliminated by the mere socialization and nationalization of profits and governmental planning. Therefore, Marx's criticism in his early writings is still valid, and applies equally well to socialist and communist countries. It is no accident that these earlier ideas about alienation have been recently revived, especially under the influ-

ence of existentialist thought, and that the critique of the young
Marx has become the fountainhead of a much broader critique of
industrial and technological society in either its capitalist or its
communist form.[15]

UTILITARIAN HEDONISM

Utilitarian hedonism expanded the naturalistic basis of Adam
Smith's interpretation of economic action by relating it to the
pleasure principle. Adam Smith explained the acquisition of more
and more money as the natural pursuit of economic self-interest.
It was an innate human propensity. The utilitarians saw it as
following from a broader natural principle that impels man to
seek pleasure and avoid pain. These two interpretations are very
close; however, the utilitarians put more stress on the teleological
and purposive aspect of action; in their formulation, the pleasure
principle functions less as a biological cause than as an end and a
purpose (this is also one of the differences between the utilitarian
and the Freudian version of this principle). By interpreting the
striving for "pleasure" as rooted in human nature, they provided for
a naturalistic and seemingly empirical theory of human behavior.

At the same time, however, the concepts of pleasure and
happiness, as used by the utilitarians, contained a substantive moral
philosophy, a belief system. They included in their definition of
pleasure most of the virtues and character traits required by the
market system. In other words, they were hiding a value system
behind the screen of a naturalistic philosophy. They tried to combine objective and purely instrumental reason in the same system
of thought. On the one hand, they used the term "pleasure," which
seems to imply a purely subjective relative concept of the satisfaction of desires as far as they are pleasurable to the individual. On
the other hand, they interpreted as pleasurable many things that
man in industrial capitalism was supposed to strive for. They projected into the term "pleasure" a normative content which was

---

[15] See Jürgen Habermas, *Theorie und Praxis* (Neuwied am Rhein und Berlin:
Verlag Luchterhand, 1963), pp. 261 ff.

largely identical with the bourgeois virtues of their time. Thus, their system of thought and values oscillated between objective and subjective instrumental reason.[16]

The idea of happiness discussed by philosophers from Aristotle to Dewey refers to matters of ultimate concern, the supreme good, the supreme value. This is not what we mean by utilitarian hedonism. We are referring to the philosophical tradition and the corresponding social orientation which replaced the acquisitive philosophy of classical economics based on the labor theory of value. This replacement was accompanied by a relativization and subjectivization of the ends and goals of life in general and of economic action in particular. The adoption of the pleasure principle was beset with the basic problem of all individualistic social philosophies: how can a society or economy which considers the satisfaction of *individual* needs as the ultimate goal arrive at a *social* value system which can become the basis of a social order? No social order is possible without any common values. A system in which the satisfaction of the purely subjective and random goals of individuals is the supreme goal must end in anarchy.

This problem was circumvented in the earlier phase of capitalism by rationalistic and ascetic restraint. Individual desires were tamed by methodical impulse control. This restraint lost ground when the belief in its religious foundations vanished. The attainment of pleasure and avoidance of pain became the ultimate guides for human behavior, and pleasure and pain were interpreted along entirely subjective lines. Thus, a powerful trend was set into motion which was destined to undermine the system and unleash disintegrating forces.

The utilitarian hedonism of the nineteenth century avoided the destructive effects of the pleasure principle by defining it very narrowly. Pleasure as the utilitarians saw it became almost identical with the traditional values of Western society and included a good deal of rationalistic and ascetic restraint. However, by choosing pleasure as the ultimate guide for human action, and individual subjective pleasurable happiness as the ultimate concern, utilitarian

---

[16] For an excellent summary of hedonist and utilitarian ideas see V. J. McGill, *The Idea of Hapiness* (New York: Frederick A. Praeger, 1967), chaps. 6 and 10.

hedonism prepared the way for the unfettered veneration of the pleasure principle and its present-day manifestations.

Bentham, Mill and the economists influenced by the utilitarian philosophers could not really take seriously the idea that pleasure (understood as the release of all restraints) could be the supreme guiding principle of all action. They had to reinterpret pleasure in such a way as to make the striving for it compatible with the behavior of men living under the new market system and in Western civilized society. Thus, from the very outset there is in utilitarian hedonism an antinomy between unrestrained subjective pleasure and the rationalistic moral restraints of industrial capitalism.

The terms used by this school are already indicative of this conflict and this antinomy. Pleasure, happiness and utility are used by Bentham synonymously; but they do not necessarily mean the same thing. Aristotle made a distinction between pleasure and happiness and rejected pleasure defined as voluptuary satisfactions as the highest good.[17] The term happiness as used in classical philosophy since Aristotle implied some ultimate good. It was identified with virtue by Plato and with pleasure by the Epicureans. By linking it with pleasure the utilitarians tried to invest the satisfaction of subjective desires of a more or less sensuous nature with the sanctity of the supreme good. In this respect they used precedents from classical philosophical tradition. Epictetus (and actually all the Greco-Roman philosophers) believed that happiness depends on the ratio of satisfied and unsatisfied desires.[18] Epictetus, however, believed in the method of "contraction" to attain happiness, to attain satisfaction by reducing one's desires. This avenue is completely rejected by the nineteenth-century utilitarians, especially by Bentham in his critque of asceticism. To Bentham asceticism is ludicrous; it approves action which diminishes pleasure or increases misery.[19]

This demonstrates that the utilitarian concept of happiness

[17] McGill, *The Idea of Happiness*, p. 13, quoting Aristotle, *Nichomachian Ethics*, 1097 b 1-6.

[18] McGill, *loc. cit.*, pp. 6, 54.

[19] McGill, *ibid.* Jeremy Bentham, *Principles of Morals and Legislation* (New York: Hafner Publishing Co., 1948), chap. II, pp. 8 ff.

and pleasure is related to the situation of man in industrial capitalism. Bentham's rejection of asceticism (although Epictetus shows that it is logically and psychologically compatible with the pursuit of happiness) reflects the modern acquisitive attitude, the activistic striving for *more and more* "satisfaction." Here, satisfaction as such is not the aim of action; it could be attained by the curbing of desires. It is *more and more* satisfaction which is interpreted as pleasure and as happiness, quite in line with pecuniary aggrandizement and acquisition, the ideals of industrial capitalism. Bentham repeated the restrictive interpretation of economic self-interest of Adam Smith. Obviously reduction of desires would be as detrimental to capitalism as a target income; they would interfere with the aim of acquisitive aggrandizement. This conflict between acquisition on the one hand, and traditional or ascetic attitudes toward wants, desires and consumption on the other hand was a problem in the transition from the preindustrial to industrial society; and it is becoming a problem again in the affluent society. From both, the preindustrial and the postindustrial affluent-society point of view, the striving for more and more, be it property or consumers' goods, assumes an irrational character; and "asceticism" or, at least, moderation in acquisition and consumption becomes more rational than the striving for more and more. That Bentham rejects every form of asceticism reflects the socioeconomic orientation of his time.

Pleasure in the narrowest sense refers to drives and instincts and to sensual pleasure. The pleasure principle points to the orientation of industrial man toward a full actualization of all instincts and drives. It presages the Freudian and the animalistic sensualistic trends in our time. However, the utilitarians may have understood that this interpretation would ultimately destroy industrial society. Therefore, they had to reinterpret pleasure in terms of Western values. One only has to turn the pages of Bentham's *Principles of Morals and Legislation* to see how pleasure and pain become something quite different from what these terms imply in common language. Every virtue and every ideal that was embraced in Western Occidental thought, and still retained in the nineteenth century, was projected into the concept of pleasure and happiness.

J. S. Mill believed that not to follow the will of God is "unpleasant." The utilitarians believed that morality was instrumental to happiness although not constitutive for it. Virtue according to Mill became a part of happiness.[20] Paley, one of the theological utilitarians, identified the submission to the will of God with private happiness: "Private happiness is our motive . . . the will of God is our rule." [21]

An important intellectual instrument in the rationalization of pleasure and in identifying happiness with the moral and religious precepts of society was the idea that long-run pleasure, indeed eternal pleasure was the determinant of action. In this way Berkeley managed to include into the pleasure principle the striving for eternal bliss.[22] This procedure was also used in the modification of the concept of interest by calling it enlightened and long-run interest. Through this modification every virtue, every moral and other restraint required by industrial society could be projected into the idea of pleasure: in order to attain long-run satisfaction, moral restraint and prudence in the present are necessary. This led, of course, to a complete reversal of the literal meaning of the pleasure principle. When Bentham enumerates what influences sensibility to pleasure and pain, he mentions first health, strength, hardiness and bodily imperfections; and then knowledge, intellectual capacity, firmness of mind, moral and religious sensibility, and so forth. McGill adds: "Here we find all the factors essential or favorable to happiness enumerated by Aristotle, except virtuous activity . . . and contemplation. Contemplation seems to be a clear omission." [23] Obviously Bentham intended to define happiness as the realization of all the moral precepts of his society; the omission of contemplation reflects its activistic bias.

Thus, in utilitarianism we find an antinomy between the pleasure principle and its reinterpretation in terms of moral repressions. The basic antinomy between the instinctual sensuous goals of the individual and social values is obliterated in thought

20 McGill, *The Idea of Happiness,* pp. 175–76, 179.
21 *Ibid.,* p. 130.
22 *Ibid.,* p. 131.
23 *Ibid.,* p. 132.

by using synonymously pleasure, happiness, religious beliefs, virtues and moral restraints.

The term *utility* shows another aspect of this antinomy. In his *Principles*, Bentham states:

"The word utility does not so clearly point to the ideas of pleasure and pain as the words happiness and felicity do; nor does it lead us to the consideration of the number of interests affected; to the . . . formation of the standard . . . of right and wrong . . ." [24] Bentham feels here that one can talk about utility only in the relation between things and one individual, and that the concept of utility is subjective and instrumental: things are useful to individuals, therefore their value is purely subjective. Their utility to individuals is determined by innumerable individual motivations and aspirations; therefore utility cannot be the basis of objective standards for what is right or wrong. Again, we find here this oscillation between the idea of utility and pleasure, based on subjective reason, and implying a repression of the normative dimension on the one hand, and the desire to arrive at objective moral normative standards on the other hand.

Utilitarians tried to bridge the gap between subjectivism and the desire for objective standards also by the idea that pleasures of individuals are quantifiable and have a common denominator and by the principle of the greatest happiness of the greatest number. Bentham's utilitarianism is distinguished from antique hedonism by its "universalistic" and collectivistic character. Its classical predecessor, Epicureanism, believed in the complete subjectivity of pleasure: "My pleasure is good for me, and yours is good for you, and the pleasures of different individuals do not add up to a grand total of pleasure." [25] Bentham's ultimate good, however, was the greatest pleasure of the greatest number which requires the quantitative homogeneity of the pleasures of individuals and the possibility of adding them up. The idea of the greatest pleasure of the greatest number is a device to translate the erratic, spontaneous, subjective desires of individuals into a social order. In order that fulfillment of the completely subjective, spontaneous, temporary, erratic, emo-

---

[24] Bentham, *Principles*, p. 1, n. 1.
[25] McGill, *op. cit.*, p. 120.

tional needs and desires of many individuals should not result in chaos, utilitarianism treats the desires of many individuals as devoid of any qualitative differences. It is assumed that there are no qualitative differences between the various pleasures of one and the same person and between pleasures of different persons. "Provided the quantity of pleasure is the same, pushpin is as good as poetry, and the satisfaction of the enlightened statesman has no intrinsic advantage over that of the criminal" says Bentham.[26] This approach is the source of most of what ails us today: the complete absence of moral standards and the view that individual "interests" are qualitatively equal and can only be compared on a quantitative basis. However, this point of view makes it possible to add up the satisfactions of individuals to a social sum total, to translate the pleasures of many individuals into utility for society as a whole. These concepts still underlie most ideas about social goals in modern economics, such as economic growth and welfare.

The other device by which utilitarianism arrives at a social order is the principle of the greatest pleasure (happiness) of the greatest number which also rests on the quantification of subjective utilities. It is used to define as a social goal the maximization of the pleasure or happiness of the majority. The importance of this intellectual device for Western society cannot be overstressed. It makes it possible to justify the oppression, repression, exploitation of, and discrimination against minority groups because this may maximize the pleasure and satisfaction of the majority. The principle of the greatest happiness of the greatest number could justify the genocide of Kulaks and Jews for the sake of the pleasure, happiness of and utility for the majority. If one would assume qualitative differences between desires and individuals, not one single death could be justified even if it established law and order for the majority; there would be no common yardstick for comparison. The quantification of satisfactions and the principle of the greatest happiness of the greatest number are the cornerstones of democracy and majority rule, and of the free market system. The idea of optimum allocation of resources and of the sovereignty of the

---

[26] *Ibid.*, p. 123.

majority of consumers developed by neoclassical economic theory rests on these two principles. The inner restraints necessary for work, production and saving are justified by the needs of the majority to whose value system the deviant minorities are forced to adjust. Every restraint made necessary by technology, bureaucracy and mass organizations can be justified by the majority principle as long as the majority considers the goals of technology and production and its organizational requirements in their interest. The majority principle is also the cornerstone of the modern political system. That this system is today rocking from the attacks of deviant minorities shows the importance of this principle, and is, at the same time, a symptom of its disintegration. The problem of this society and of rebellious youth today is: how can a minority make its voice heard and its interests considered in a system which is based on majority rule? The advocacy of marches, demonstrations, riots and the defense of violence and guerrilla warfare owes its origin to this situation; the idea is that only through demonstrations or through violence can minorities and their interests become visible in the public realm and participate in politics. Whatever lack of merits these ideas have, they are the obvious result of the majority principle.

As we have pointed out, however, this line of reasoning so prevalent among the rebellious minorities of today holds true only if the majority principle is interpreted by relativistic, subjective instrumental reason as an instrument of expediency. If the voice of the majority is the voice of "God," that is, of objective reason, then the majority can appeal to objectively valid standards and can demand their recognition by the minorities. If the majority principle is looked upon merely as a relativistic device so that the interests of a larger number of people are satisfied, the minorities can rightly claim that their own interests should also be considered. In this case, they may be justified in using demonstrations and even violence to attain the satisfaction of their interests if everything else has failed. Value relativism and the repression of objective reason breed violence. This is the essence of the struggle that rages today in our universities, in the ghettos and in politics. Take rebellious students: If one can claim general validity for the standards of traditional education, cleanliness, civility and polite language and behavior, the majority would have the right to demand the observation of these standards from rebellious students. This demand becomes questionable if there is doubt about the "goodness" of these standards in the minds of the majority. The faculties against whom students rebel also harbor silent doubts about the relevance of what they are teaching. This makes them compliant to even the most arbitrary demands. It is significant that academic rebellion is directed mostly against the social sciences and humanities and less against the natural sciences (except for their political and military uses), probably because there are fewer doubts about the validity of technical and scientific education than about education in the humanities and social sciences. Doubts exist in the fields that deal with the value system of our society, and there the doubts are harbored by rebels and defenders of these values alike. Militant blacks demand black courses in sociology, economics, history and psychology, but not in business and in technical, vocational education. Wherever objective reason seems to justify the existing institutions, there is no attempt to attack them; the rebellion is confined to those fields in which relativism and doubts have undermined the belief in the validity of what is passed on through education.

NEOCLASSICAL ECONOMICS

The neoclassical school of economics, whose "founder" was the British economist Alfred Marshall (1842–1924), tried to combine an objective theory of value built on the cost of production with a subjective value theory based on utility. This approach has greatly influenced British and American economic writing and thinking; his theory is still the center not only of most textbook-writing in economics but of most economic reasoning about price theory. In general, the neoclassical school translated the philosophical and moral system of classicism and utilitarianism into "quantitative, scientific" language. In the process, the traces of objective reason and the ethical content of the system became more and more obscured. Impulse-control, which was so important in the Protestant-Puritan moral philosophy, had already been pushed into the background in classical and utilitarian economic thought; however, it is still part of the neoclassical scheme but there impulse-control became more and more a by-product of the purposive rationalism to which the utilitarian pleasure principle had been reduced. Its "pleasurable" felicific aspects were neglected. Economic behavior was considered "virtuous" if it was based on expedient rationality aiming at efficiency. The latter was defined as maximization of monetary or consumption gains. This scheme was treated, in imitation of the natural sciences, in a quantitative way; the utilitarian calculus was first refined by neoclassical economics, and later by present-day logistic model-building, into a fine art of implicitly normative directives "more geometrico and mathematico." Rational efficiency and maximization of gains became moral imperatives in technology and in economic practice and theory, regardless of the results of "efficiency," of what is being maximized.

However, the neoclassical school of economics was confronted with the same problem as utilitarianism: how to combine subjective wishes, desires and wants with the restraints and the discipline necessary in the market economy. This problem arose because of the shift in economic thought from an objective theory of value which considered the amount of labor and factors of production or their costs as the determinant of economic value to the subjective yardstick of utility and consumers' demand. This was a transition from a central belief system, from objective reason and objective standards of value, to instrumental, subjective reason in economic thought. In the labor theory of value according to which a good has value because of the amount of labor used in its production (and in some versions of this theory because of its cost of production), an objective standard was used; the value of a good was based on something inherent in the good, something that was used and expended during the process of production (the amount of labor or the costs of production). In the theories which explained economic value and prices by the utility of the good for those who demand it, a subjective yardstick, extraneous to the good, was used to explain value. The subjective explanation of economic value based on utility took the form of the so-called marginal utility theory of value which was independently developed by the English economist William Stanley Jevons (1835–1882), the Austrian Karl Menger (1840–1921) and the Frenchman Léon Walras (1834–1910). The value of a good was assumed to depend on its utility for consumers; but its price is determined by the relation between its supply and the demand for it, the so-called marginal utility of a unit of the good. Even if a good is very useful to consumers, if its supply is abundant in relation to the demand for it, its price will be low because each unit of this abundant supply has a relatively small value (a low marginal utility). Thus, air under normal conditions, although essential for survival, has no value or price because an infinitely large supply is available.

It is instructive to examine the validity of the two theories, the objective labor theory of value and the subjective marginal utility theory of value. Most Western economists today are inclined to believe that the labor theory is wrong and the marginal utility theory is right. However, if one puts oneself into the position of an observer during the Industrial Revolution, one can see how actual historical experiences determine ideas and may have supported the validity of the labor theory of value. During the first half of the nineteenth century, the most striking phenomenon was the great increase in productivity per man hour because of technological improvements. This often led to an increase in the supply of goods and a fall in their prices. The facts of this situation confirm both the labor theory of value and the marginal utility theory: (1) The amount of labor time used in the production of, for example, a yard of cloth was reduced because of the use of machinery; (2) therefore, the supply of cloth increased in relation to the demand and (3) the price of a yard of cloth declined. This is a chain of causation composed of various links. The labor theory of value looked at links (1) and (3); the utility theory at links (2) and (3). One cannot call either theory right or wrong; they both are incomplete, because each leaves out one link in the chain of causation. The increase in supply was caused by an increase in the productivity of labor. The labor theory is, therefore, applicable in this particular case although it leaves out a link in the chain of causation. It is false only if it is used as a general universally valid principle and divorced from the circumstances which caused its formulation.

The shift from an objective to a subjective value theory in the second half of the nineteenth century was related to a change in the character of the economy. The increase in capital equipment, the progress of technology and the increase in output created the problem of finding marketing outlets for a capital-rich economic system with a high productive capacity. This explains the change of emphasis away from the objective, production-mindedness of the classicists. The marginalist and neoclassical schools partly reflected and partly foreshadowed this trend by moving the subjective element of wants, desires, need satisfaction and demand into the center of economic thought, thereby taking seriously the utilitarian hedonistic approach. Demand moved into the center of discussion and consumers' motives and actions were analyzed.

This subjectivism was, however, thoroughly blended with economic rationality. The turn toward subjective needs, utility, happiness and individual desires brought to the fore a hidden problem of the industrial economy: the existence of human inclinations incompatible with the type of conduct which the economic system required—for example, the disinclination to work, the resistance to activism, the desire for passivity, contemplation, enjoyment of nature, art and the senses, the unwillingness to pursue long-run goals in a systematic, consistent fashion, to act deliberately and calculatedly, to repress capricious, impulsive behavior. If satisfaction of human desires was the ultimate goal, much of economic activity was endangered by the fact that the industrial system and the exchange economy permit only the satisfaction of a narrowly circumscribed type of need: those which can be satisfied by acquisition of money and goods through work and exchange in the market; and they can be satisfied only in a way which conflicts with many "noneconomic" human propensities; other desires are repressed. The classical economists circumvented this, not only by the fiction of the invisible hand and of the natural harmony of interests, but also by their rigid adherence to a value system which considered objective factors such as more and more production and acquisition as ultimate goals. The shift toward subjectivity removed this possibility. Alfred Marshall provided for a counterweight against purely relativistic and anarchic subjectivity in his emphasis on economic rationality. He represents economic rationalism as an ideal and, at the same time, as the ultimate result of economic laws. He tried to show that consumer and industry behavior can be understood with the help of models of rational economic behavior and that this type of conduct will have long-run beneficial results.

The value symbol of rational economic man became the focal point of economic thinking. It was combined with an idealization of the activistic mode of life. Wants are subordinated to activities. An element of the work ethic is still retained in spite of the stress on subjective desires. Not so much satisfaction of needs but activities, directed toward the higher goals in life and toward character formation, are the ultimate ends.[27] Rational, deliberate conduct and self-control become the primary ideals.

Through this emphasis on rationality, directed toward the goal of higher activities, the danger was avoided that nonrational, impulsive, emotional elements would enter through the door of subjectivism and destroy not only the regularity of the economic laws, but also the value-orientation required for the working of the economic system. Therefore, it had to be demonstrated that rationality dominates all types of economic activity. The consumer, housewife, entrepreneur, industrial firm, saver, etc., are all represented as people who consciously balance opposing forces, values, interests in such a fashion that they maximize the total of their advantages, utility, profits, and so forth and thus aim at and reach a point of equilibrium. In all these cases the existence of inner conflicts between goals, values and impulses and between what man wants to do and what the economic system permits him to do is ignored. Conflicting drives and inclinations of a qualitatively different nature are reduced to a common quantitative denominator, so that conscious comparison of relative quantities of gain and loss can show the way to a clear-cut decision, maximizing benefits and

[27] T. Parsons, *The Structure of Social Action* (Glencoe, Ill.: The Free Press, 1949), pt. II, chap. IV.

equilibrating opposing forces. Rational economic conduct, maximization of gains and equilibrium become symbols of economic harmony.

This model of rational economic conduct is supposed to be an explanatory pattern for human economic behavior, but it is, at the same time, a normative directive, an ideal of how economic men in the market economy should behave. The traces of the Puritan economic ethic are still visible in the writings of Marshall which are the source of what today is called microeconomics. (Microeconomics is the examination of the laws and principles which rule the determination of prices on specific markets, and consists mostly of an analysis of how changes in supply and demand influence prices on a free market. It is distinguished from macroeconomics which deals with events affecting the entire economy such as inflation and deflation, expansion and contraction of economic activity, prosperity and depression.) For Marshall, maximization is clearly an ideal and a moral obligation; economic rationality has not only a descriptive but a normative character.

"And in a money economy, good management is shown by so adjusting the margins of suspense on each line of expenditure that the marginal utility of a shilling's worth of goods on each line shall be the same. And this result each one will attain by constantly watching to see whether there is anything on which he is spending so much that he would gain by taking a little away from that line of expenditiure and putting it on some other line." [28]

This scheme of conscious allocation of expenditure for the attainment of maximization of utility (called "equalization at the margin") is not merely advice on good business management but an ideal for economic man, prescribing how he should allocate and distribute his time, energy and income to various ends so as to maximize his total utility, pleasure and happiness. It establishes an inseparable interrelation between instrumental economic, means-ends rationality and impulse control. The pattern of this rationality is taken from technology and business. Only in technology is there a clear-cut maximization goal: either to produce the greatest

---

[28] Alfred Marshall, *Principles of Economics,* 8th ed. (London: Macmillan and Co., 1920), p. 118.

amount of products with a given amount of means; or to produce a given amount of products with the smallest amounts of means. This kind of pattern makes sense in technology where both means of production and products can be physically measured and compared, where physical, technical efficiency is quantitatively measurable.

It also makes sense in business where both means of production and the results of production can be measured in terms of money and a cost-profit calculation can be undertaken. Efficiency is attained in the maximization of profits by either producing a given sales revenue with the lowest cost or by producing the highest profits with a given amount of expenditure. It is highly dubious whether such a maximization scheme can realistically be applied to the behavior of a consumer or used as a general pattern for individual behavior. Even if one accepts that all behavior is conscious, deliberate and maximizing—a patently unrealistic assumption—the scheme runs into two difficulties: one, the impossibility of reducing all ends to the same quantitative denominator so as to make them measurable and comparable; two, the impossibility of avoiding a conflict of ends. The real situation which people experience continuously is that they are torn between conflicting goals. Their decision is not based on measuring the relative advantages and deciding for the greater one; they cut through the Gordian knot of ambivalent conflict and then regret their decision. Whether somebody decides to marry the homely housewife or the comely flapper, he will afterward long for what he has sacrificed, and feel that the grass always looks greener on the other side. It is quite significant that Marshall excludes regret from his ideal of economic man. An allocation decision that causes regret later is considered as an irrational failure.[29] Allocation of time and energy, of resources and income should be based on a lifelong, permanent, lasting scale of preferences, values, goals and meanings. Book III, chapter V of Marshall's *Principles of Economics* is full of obviously moralistic advice on how a prudent consumer and householder should choose between different wants and be-

[29] *Ibid.*, p. 117.

tween present and future wants. All this advice is based on the principle of long-run steadfastness of wants which should lead to "wholesome," long-lasting enjoyment, avoid "transient luxuries" and conform to the "true" interests of the individual. The "consumption of alcohol and tobacco, and some indulgence in fashionable dress . . . by workers are commonly classed as productive consumption but strictly speaking it ought not to be." [30] All this implies a high degree of impulse-control in consumption and generally an individual behavior pattern imbued with economic rationality. This rationality receives its *substantive meaning* from impulse-control. The ideal of economic man in its neoclassical Marshallian form is not yet a completely value-empty scheme. It identifies rationality with the conquest of spontaneous, erratic, temporary, transitory impulses and temptations; these are sacrificed for a permanent, lifelong, lasting, wholesome way of life which is identical with the values of Victorian bourgeois society. Galsworthy's *Forsyte Saga*, especially the personality of Soames Forsyte, is a perfect personification of this way of life (including the detrimental effects of Victorian repression). The amalgamation of economic rationality with impulse-control performs two functions: it gives to the formalistic maximization scheme a substantive content and thus invests it with the dignity of a moral code; but it also imprisons human behavior in the iron cage of Victorian morality. The erratic, capricious, spontaneous, unconscious, instinctual human drives and proclivities are condemned, repressed and pushed into the dungeon of the irrational (to be resurrected today by various "liberation" movements). This is done summarily by the interpretation of human conduct as conscious, deliberate action and by the exclusion of all unconscious, spontaneous behavior from the economic universe of discourse: and it is done by the identification of rationality with impulse-control. The door that was slightly opened for the repressed impulses by the pleasure principle of the utilitarians was closed again by identifying pleasure with the goals attainable through economic rationality. This pattern of thought, however, merely hides the conflict between

---

[30] *Ibid.*, p. 70.

the irrational impulses implied in the subjectivistic concept of consumers' wants and the impulse-controlling scheme of economic
rationality.

Marshall enlarged the maximization scheme of individual rational conduct to cover the entire economic system. Not only individuals maximize but so do firms, markets and industries, and the
entire economy. Everywhere quantified advantages and disad-
vantages are measured, weighed, and decisions made which supposedly lead to a *collective* maximization point and equilibrium.
The market balances supply and demand. The industry arrives
at an equilibrium at a price which covers the cost of production of
all firms whose output is necessary to satisfy the demand at that
price. But if it is doubtful that the individual consumer acts consciously and deliberately to reach a measurable maximization point,
it is even more doubtful concerning a collectivity like a market
or an industry. Who is the consciously maximizing individual?
How does it happen that the equilibrium of the market occurs "as
if" there were an "invisible hand" that guides the market price
toward an equilibrium position? In *The Psychology of Economics*
(pp. 194 ff.) I point out that Marshall could prove the establishment of an equilibrium price only through assuming that all buyers
and sellers had perfect knowledge of each other's intentions. This
implies a personification of the market which then acts like one
person who knows his own preferences and consciously tries to
maximize his utility. The scheme of rational economic conduct is
applied to the market where prices are established as if a rational
individual tries to establish an equilibrium between efforts and
satisfactions, supply and demand. The ethical code of rational,
maximizing, economic man becomes the law of the market—an
obvious attempt to ground a normative scheme of values in facts,
thereby justifying these values.

The same scheme is applied to the entire economy in the concept of optimum allocation of resources, which is supposed to be
brought about by the free market and to lead toward a collective
maximization of social utility and welfare. This idea was developed
on the continent by Vilfredo Pareto (1848–1923) and Léon
Walras. However, Marshall's *Principles* contains the basic ideas

for an optimum allocation approach (in his analysis of long-run normal price, *Principles*, Book V, which was elaborated by A. C. Pigou in his *Economics of Welfare* and by modern welfare economics). Such factors of production as land, labor and capital are guided in their uses by changes in consumer's demand in such a way that social utility and welfare will be maximized. This concept of optimum allocation of resources projects the value system of economic rationalism into the entire economy. The economy is interpreted as striving toward an equilibrating maximization point. The ideal of economic rationalism with its subjection of impulses is rediscovered as a scientific law, applicable equally to individuals and to the economy. If industrial man can be made to believe that the entire economy behaves like he is supposed to behave, it will confirm his faith in the validity of his conduct. A repressive value system is thus legitimized by a belief in subjective utility, rational maximization, impulse-control and economic equilibrium.

4

The Triumph of Value-Relativism
in Economic Thought

ETHICAL RELATIVISM IN ECONOMIC THOUGHT

The schools of economic thought so far examined—classical economics, utilitarianism, and neoclassicism—still retained traces of objective reason—a belief system—together with impulse-control. These traces evaporated fast with the progress of industrial capitalism. The development from objective encompassing reason to technical instrumental and subjective reason transcends economics; it accompanied the general disintegration of traditional values in Western civilization. Reason became formalized, desubstantiated and emptied of all normative content. Gone is Adam Smith's value distinction between productive versus unproductive labor. Gone are the Marshallian exhortations toward prudence and life planning and restraint in consumption. Gone are J. S. Mill's praises of solitude, and his warnings that nature should not be completely destroyed and eliminated by production and that there is "as much room for improving the art of living and much more likelihood of its being improved when minds ceased to be engrossed by the art of getting on." [1] The value-relativism, accompanied by a complete

---

[1] John Stuart Mill, *Principles of Political Economy* (London: Longmans Green, 1929), pp. 750-51.

formalization of rationality without any content, has been best expressed by Lionel L. Robbins:

> So far as we [economists] are concerned our economic subjects can be pure egoists, pure altruists, pure ascetics, pure sensualists . . . Our deductions do not provide any justification for saying that caviar is an economic good and carrion a disutility . . . Individual valuations . . . are outside the sphere of economic uniformity . . . from the point of view of economic analysis these things constitute the irrational element in our universe of discourse.[2]

One could not formulate the position of value-relativism more succinctly. We find here a complete subjectivization and relativization of individual economic goals. No moral judgment, no objective value standard should be applied by the economist to individual preferences which determine the demand for goods. The realm of values is expelled from the realm of reason. Values are not only subjective, pluralistic, relative and different for different individuals; they are also irrational and not amenable to reasonable discussion. Value-neutrality is pushed to the extreme and becomes complete value-emptiness.

This standpoint, however, is ultimately repudiated by Robbins in his statement:

> And thus, in the last analysis, economics does depend . . . on an ultimate valuation—the affirmation that rationality and ability to choose with knowledge is desirable. If irrationality, if the surrender to the blind forces of external stimuli and uncoordinated impulse at every moment is a good to be preferred above all others, then it is true that the *raison d'être* of economics disappears.[3]

Here, *formal rationality* empty of content and interpreted as the maximization of subjective utility whatever it consists of, becomes the ultimate *ideal*. It is formal maximizing rationality for formal maximizing rationality's sake. Acting according to a conscious, rational, preconceived plan, with conscious, deliberate weighing of alternatives and conscious choice between them in such a way as

---

[2] Lionel Robbins, *An Essay on the Nature and Significance of Economic Science* (London: Macmillan, 1946), pp. 95, 106.
[3] *Ibid.*, p. 157.

to maximize some subjective utility which can consist in the maximization of *any* individual desire, becomes the ultimate guide to rational action. If one would take this scheme seriously, a rationally planned deliberate murder would also conform to this ideal. According to this pattern of content-empty, formal rationality, the concentration camps would be the acme of expedient technical rationality. They were efficiently organized to commit genocide. The goal—genocide as the "final solution"—could, under Robbins' definition, not be subject to any "rational" judgment by economists; it would—in the truest sense of the term— be part of the "irrational element" in the universe of rational discourse.

Without in any way accusing Lord Robbins (and the long line of economists who, before and after him, have adopted this relativistic attitude) of any criminal intent, it is obvious that this kind of value-relativism leads to what one could call the Eichmann complex (or the repudiation of the Nuremberg principle). The Nuremberg and the Eichmann trials centered around the question whether moral laws and principles have precedence over the commands of superiors. The real question—far transcending economics and even the Nazi atrocities—is inherent in the Western abandonment of objective reason and in the cutting off of value-judgments from reason. If the goal of genocide—like any goal of economic or other action—is an irrational element in the rational universe of discourse, Eichmann and others of the same ilk could safely ignore the immorality of this goal and retreat into their rational pursuit of genocide. If formal, maximizing rationality is "good" regardless of its content, and if rationality exhausts itself in the efficient pursuit of any goal regardless of its origin and content, there is no principle from which one could deduce the duty to examine the goal itself. This question arises frequently: conscientious objection, the protest against the war in Vietnam, the war- and death-related services of universities and scientists, tax payments for destruction, investing in the stock of firms which produce for war or practice discrimination—all these situations raise the question of applying objective reason to value-judgments. Quite apart from the logical difficulties which this problem poses, the practical effects of value-relativism are clear: it leads to nihilism in respect to values and weakens the moral fiber and civil courage of individuals.

There is a certain hypocrisy in our condemning the Nazi atrocities of an Eichmann and pretending that his value-relativism is foreign to the rest of industrial and democratic society. After all, a concentration camp differs from a factory only by the degree of "goodness" or "badness" of its ultimate goal. The efficient production of thermonuclear weapons, of nerve gases and materials of biological warfare can be compared to a concentration camp; the similarity in these situations is that the goal can be considered as morally reprehensible whereas the pursuit is carried out with the utmost efficiency and rationality. This antinomy between "bad, irrational" ends and "good, rational" efficient means is a characteristic of industrial capitalism. It could be said that this society has turned the slogan that the ends justify the means, to read that (rational) means justify (bad and irrational) ends. Everything that science and technology makes possible, that is everything that can be accomplished with what passes for rationality and efficiency in modern society, is permitted, indeed is justified; because it can be done efficiently and profitably, it is assumed that it should be done, regardless of its negative moral implications.

Value-relativism in regard to economic conduct also aggravates the problem any individualistic social philosophy has in arriving at a tenable concept of a social order or common good. It makes insoluble the problem of coordinating individual and social goals, individual and public interests. There must be a common belief and value system from which rules for individual and social conduct and goals are derived; otherwise there will be an unbridgeable antinomy between individual and social goals. In such a case only external compulsion can keep society together. Individual freedom and a social philosophy which considers individuals as the sovereigns of society can only be maintained if these individuals have internalized a value system which induces them to act as the social and economic system requires them to act. A value-relativistic social philosophy, trying to legitimize any and all individual desires regardless of their content, will make social cooperation and cohesion impossible.

INDIVIDUAL AND SOCIAL ECONOMIC WELFARE

The classics identified economic growth with welfare, a concrete ideal which rests on the assumption of a harmony of individual and social goals. This identification, however, proved to be impossible when economics shifted from an objective to a subjective value theory. Subjective individual satisfactions can only be integrated into social goals if these goals are defined in a purely formal way. This is precisely the idea that underlies modern welfare economics.

It is not my intention to give a technical presentation of modern welfare economics.[4] What I want to do is uncover its implicit image of man and society because this image clearly shows a pattern of alienation from the normative, moral dimension and the complete abandonment of reason as applied to ends. What matters here is the social philosophy which underlies this construct of economic welfare. Such a social philosophy has to deal with the following problems: (1) What are the goals of individuals? (2) What are the goals of society? (3) How are the two interrelated?

The classical school identified individual and social economic goals: both consist of an increase in production. But Adam Smith justified *individual* acquisitiveness by its *social* beneficiality. Welfare economics chooses the opposite way: it tries to derive social goals from the sum total of individual satisfactions. The classical school identified individual and social economic goals by defining them in *objective* terms, as an increase in total production. The subjectivistic approach tries to reach the same result by interpreting the social goal in individualistic subjective terms. Welfare economics eliminates the social and moral content of the concept of economic welfare and finds welfare only in an increase of the welfare of the individuals; but the welfare of individuals is also denuded of any objective content and defined in purely value-empty terms of formal maximization of subjective "utility" which,

---

4 For the interested layman the books by I. M. D. Little, *A Critique of Welfare Economics*, 2nd ed. (New York: Oxford University Press, 1957), and Hla Myint, *Theories of Welfare Economics* (Cambridge, Mass.: Harvard University Press, 1948), could serve as an introduction, although they contain a good deal of technical material.

at least in theory, can include anything that the individual desires. No idea of the individual good, the "common good," the "public interest" or the good as such, no concept of right and wrong, is left in the modern concepts of common welfare. The economy is viewed as an agglomeration of individuals, each with a multitude of individual subjective desires which they are supposed to satisfy to the maximum possible degree. The assumption is that *social* welfare would be increased if the satisfaction of some *individuals* can be increased without decreasing the satisfaction of other individuals.[5] "In its simplest version, the fundamental proposition of welfare economics states that any economic change that makes someone better off without making anyone worse off is a desirable change from the point of view of group or social welfare. In a somewhat more sophisticated version, the proposition states that any economic change that results in the situation whereby the beneficiaries from the change can compensate those who lose from the change and still be better off themselves is a desirable change from the point of view of social welfare" (the so-called Pareto principle).[6]

Thus, the definition of what increases *social* welfare is traced back to what increases the welfare of individuals. The social philosophy of welfare economics is derived from the individualistic libertarian principle that "nothing is good for society unless it is held to be good by the individuals who form this society." [7] This formulation is incomplete. It should read "Unless it is held to be good by them regardless of whether it is good for society as a whole." The libertarian principle in its value-relativistic form as used in modern welfare economics does not distinguish between the common good and the good for individuals. This is overlooked by the otherwise instructive work of S. T. Worland,[8] who wants to prove that the two are quite compatible. Scholastic

---

[5] For a relatively nontechnical presentation of the concepts of modern welfare economics, see S. T. Worland, *Scholasticism and Welfare Economics* (Notre Dame, Ind., and London: University of Notre Dame Press, 1967), chap. V.

[6] K. G. Saini, "A Critique of Affluence: Mishan on the Cost of Economic Growth," *Journal of Economic Issues*, vol. II, no. 4 (December, 1968), 399.

[7] Mishan, *The Cost of Economic Growth* (London: The Staples Press, 1967), p. 45.

[8] *Scholasticism and Welfare Economics*.

Thomism had a central value and belief system based on revelation and objective reason. Although it favors private property for the sake of personal incentives, it emphasizes objective ethical criteria in individual economic behavior—a person has to lead a virtuous life—and it emphasizes a social ethical ideal in terms of the "common good of society as a whole . . . the furthering of the general welfare of the whole community rather than the individual good of any particular member of a group within society." [9]

In welfare economics, the last weak remnant of an objective good, an objective idea of what is right might be found in the idea that nobody should be made better off if this would make somebody else worse off. Why is harm to others morally condemned? There is no basis for such a moral judgment in a purely individualistic, subjectivistic content-empty ethics. A purely individualistic social philosophy can only result in a society in which divergent individual interests oppose each other, a power struggle results and leads to some sort of a precarious compromise. Classical economics denied the conflict of interests through the ideal of an increasing individual and social product, and by hiding behind the screen of a natural harmony of interests brought about by the "invisible hand." The empty formality of welfare economics closes this avenue of escape. The postulate that nobody should gain from a welfare measure at the expense of anybody else is a last residue of traditional ethics.

Economists have complicated their approach to *social* welfare by combining the optimum position of the economy (where no further improvement is possible without damaging somebody) with marginal cost pricing.[10] The optimum position of the economy is defined in terms of certain relationships between the costs of production and the prices of goods (in technical language: the marginal costs of all factors of production, labor, raw materials, machines, must be equal to their prices). This makes the optimum position dependent on the existing price and wage structure and on all the institutions which determine this structure. It also depends on the existence of a narrowly defined free enter-

---

[9] Worland, *loc. cit.*, p. 36.
[10] Mishan, *The Cost of Economic Growth*, pp. 46 ff.

prise system: an economy composed of many small firms none of which has any power to influence prices by its own isolated action, competing with each other through pricing, underbidding each other as sellers, and outbidding each other as buyers. It also requires the perfect mobility of productive factors and firms and the perfect knowledge by buyers and sellers of all present and future market conditions so that they can move from one market to the other at a moment's notice, in pursuit of higher gains. In such an "ideal" economy the uncontrolled forces of the free market would move the economy into an "optimum" position in which nobody's position could be improved without harming somebody. That this model is patently abstract and does not conform to the present economic reality with large dominant firms, little price competition and imperfect knowledge of present and future market condition is widely admitted. But from this admission it merely follows that the economy will not reach an optimal position by itself, and that such a position must be brought about by government action. What is important to understand is that the idea of an optimum position, a normative postulate, grew out of an analysis of the market mechanism, of what economists consider to be the ideal type of a free enterprise system. Thus, social economic welfare is implicitly defined as a state of affairs which such a free enterprise system would bring about. It is an implicit apologetics for this economic system. Both the model of the free enterprise system and the definition of optimality—the "best" allocation of resources —reenforce each other. The clearly normative postulate of optimality is shown to be the result of the free enterprise system as defined by economic theory; and this system brings about the "common" good of optimality, thereby proving its "goodness."

In such an economy the greatest possible welfare for all depends on the existing income distribution, one of the elements which determines the existing price structure. "The relative prices of goods arise, in principle, from the pattern of demand that emerges from the distribution of income . . ." [11] Different systems of income distributions would lead to different prices and

---

[11] *Ibid.*, p. 47.

thus to different optimal economic situations composed of different collections of goods. "For each of these efficiently produced collections of goods could be made optimal best by some appropriate distribution of income." [12] *Welfare economics does not provide any basis for deciding what is an optimal distribution of income;* such a yardstick would have to be derived from a dimension outside of the economic universe of discourse. This is more than a wise division of labor between disciplines. It is an unwarranted abdication of welfare economics in view of a major problem of *economic* welfare. By no stretch of the commonsense meaning of words can one exclude the distribution of income from *economic* welfare. By this exclusion and by assuming the distribution of income as "given," welfare economics falls short of performing its task of providing rules for an ideal economy.

There are various reasons for this line of reasoning. One is an implicit bias in favor of the economic status quo.[13] Existing income distribution is not subjected to any critical, normative yardstick. Another is the individualistic, subjectivistic bias of economics in general. From the point of view of the individual, the socio-economic framework that enables him to earn and spend an income is, indeed, given and, more or less, unchangeable. His "maximization" or "optimization" decisions must take place within this given framework and consist in adjusting to it. As welfare economics takes an individualistic, subjectivistic approach, it treats the whole economy as if it were an individual which has to adjust to the existing economic structure, including its income distribution. Furthermore, welfare economics simply postulates the free market as an ideal. Social welfare is maximized if the whole economy is in an equilibrium situation that would be brought about by a completely free competitive market system. If we actually lived in such an economy, any normative guidelines for economic amelioration would be considered superfluous. Thus, welfare economics is caught in a dilemma: being an offspring of the free market philosophy it should not be concerned with normative directives for improvement at all. Being a normative discipline it

---

[12] *Ibid.*, p. 49.
[13] *Ibid.*

is forced to develop normative rules. It tries to escape from this dilemma by minimizing its normative character: one, by abandoning any concept of the good and the common good apart from the subjectively evaluated good of individuals; two, by refraining from applying any normative yardstick to income distribution.

Thus, welfare economics shows all the traits of technical, instrumental, formalized, subjectivized reason with its repression of substantial concrete morality. There is no moral principle by which the subjective interests of individuals can be restricted. The optimization pattern of welfare economics rests on the same social philosophy as value-relativistic democracy. Society is a bundle of individuals with subjective interests not subject to any restrictive normative rule; their aspirations cannot be judged to be good or bad, right or wrong, from any objective or common social point of view. The only objective rule about the common good developed by welfare economics is that welfare measures should not promote anybody's individual interest if this would hurt anybody else's interest. That is no minor admission by an individualistic discipline, the product of an individualistic society; but it is not enough to tackle the grave problems of setting priorities in an industrial and postindustrial society. These problems involve conflicts between individual interests, usually of a monetary kind, versus the good in general, or the common good in particular. Their solution requires some definition or, at least, some existential experience of the good, of an unconditional moral imperative. Such experience, emotions, feelings, ideas still exist even in our pluralistic, value-relativistic society, mostly as remnants of the Judeo-Christian tradition; but they lack any intellectual basis because of the repression of the normative by technical formalized reason. The question of the rightness or wrongness of our national priorities is continuously raised: are more armaments, more highways, more cars, and so forth more important than war against poverty and hunger, rebuilding of the slums, better education and medical care? These are ultimately moral problems, or, to accommodate those who are afraid even to use the term "moral," questions of individual and social goals. Decisions about such priorities cannot be based on the principle developed by welfare economics that one should not make anybody better off by making somebody else worse off, while leaving the definition of "better" and "worse" to the concerned individuals. There is much to be said in favor of making—through taxing and spending—the higher income groups "worse off" in order to make the poor better off. This conclusion is based on a system of morality which extols such virtues as charity, compassion and selflessness. This is also a matter of defining objectively what "better" or "worse off" means. From a "moralistic" point of view such measures are at least as important to those who give up some income and property as to those whose economic welfare would be increased. The good conscience of those who sacrifice may increase their "moral welfare," thus compensating them for the reduction of their economic welfare. Technical reasoning in economics abhors such terminology. Therefore, some economists have reasoned that an additional dollar given to the poor increases total utility and satisfaction by more than the taking away of a dollar from the rich reduces it. This kind of intellectual acrobatics shows how far technical reasoning will go in self-deception in order to avoid moral judgments. It may be true that often a poor man appreciates an additional dollar more than a rich man would deplore its loss. However, if one considers only subjective evaluation, the opposite may also be the case: A rich miser who turns around every penny many times before spending it may lose one dollar with a bleeding heart, whereas the poor profligate or an ascetic may not give a tinker's damn about one dollar more or less. Furthermore, the conclusion that a redistribution of income in favor of the poor will increase "social" satisfaction rests on the assumption that subjective utilities can be summed up and aggregated. This in turn assumes that the subjective feelings of individuals can be measured, added up and subtracted with the help of a common quantitative denominator. This kind of reasoning stems from the desperate attempt to find a nonmoral arithmetical basis for a measure which can only be justified on moral grounds. Logically untenable arguments of a purely quantitative nature have been used to avoid a moral commitment, a clear symptom of the repression of the moral dimension. Thus, no argument can be made on the basis of modern welfare economics for a redistribution of income in favor of the poor at the expense of the rich.

Based on ideas developed in the eighteenth century, economists have tried to replace the idea of the good and the common good by the concept of "long-run interest." As pointed out (pp. 75 ff.), this is a way to circumvent moral judgments and decisions. On purely logical grounds or on grounds of the subjective utility and satisfaction *of one and the same individual*, it is difficult to make a clear distinction between short- and long-run interests. For one individual such a choice seems identical with the choice between present and future satisfaction for which there is no *logical* yardstick. From a purely subjective point of view, any individual is free to prefer immediate satisfaction to providing for the future; the African tribe that feasted at harvest times and starved in between did not violate the code of economic rationality as far as it is purely subjectivistic, content-empty and formal. However, the idea of long-run interest is more than that. It postulates implicitly a concept of virtuous behavior that involves restrictions in the pursuit of immediate, subjective satisfactions. It implies the Marshallian, Victorian ideas of permanence of values and temporal consistency of goals. The individual is supposed to follow a life plan and to restrain momentary impulses. This behavior should be structured in such a way that the attainment of satisfaction is not accompanied by later regrets. These ideas are remnants of Puritan impulse-control. Calling such life goals "interests," even with the adjective "long-run," will not eliminate the element of moral restraint which they contain. The term "long-run interests" is a compromise, the result of the attempt to formulate the motives of behavior "scientifically" in purely subjectivistic terms without recourse to moral norms on the one hand, and still to retain some moral concepts, some ideas about virtues on the other hand.

Welfare economics tries to arrive at some notion of the common good with the help of the concept of "external diseconomies"; these are "the damages inflicted on other members of society in the process of producing or using certain goods which are not calculated into either their cost of production nor into their market price." [14] The use of the term "external" is significant. It betrays the segmentalized outlook of an economics which distinguishes between economic welfare in terms of the goods produced and their evaluation in the existing price and income structure, and some "external" welfare which may inconveniently be reduced by an increase in the production and use of goods. The distinction between "internal" benefits and "external" diseconomies is of a historical nature; it betrays a growing doubt about the beneficiality of an economic system which is exclusively concerned with producing and consuming more and more goods and services. The tremendous increase in the volume and variety of goods and services has made their detrimental by-products increasingly visible. However, instead of revising the entire concept of welfare to include noneconomic elements, economists wanted to save their analytical box of tools, retaining them for "internal" benefits and adjusting them for application to "external diseconomies." These diseconomies are mostly such physical "disamenities" as air and water pollution, excessive engine noise, dirt, stench, ugliness, urban sprawl, automobilization, traffic jams, etc.[15] An attempt has been made to include these external diseconomies in traditional economic analysis by transforming "private cost calculable by the producer on strict commercial principles, into social cost by adding to the private cost the value of an incidental damage inflicted on the rest of society . . ." [16] This procedure, however, completely destroys the libertarian foundation of welfare economics which rests, as shown, on the acceptance of the existing *private* market, price and income structure. It changes completely the concept of cost from something the individual entrepreneur has to defray, to include the *social* effects of his actions that violate the *common good*, and imposes these social costs on the private entrepreneur. This may be a legitimate procedure: the private firm should perhaps pay for these social ill-effects; what is important is to realize that a moral element, a concept of the common good has been reintroduced in

---

14 *Ibid.*, p. 51.
15 *Ibid.*, p. 55.
16 *Ibid.*, p. 54.

an intellectual framework which, in the past, has excluded such a concept. Here, the concept of the common good, necessary to judge what is a damage to society, is smuggled in by simply trans-substantiating private into social cost. This is a case in which a change in quantity amounts to a change in quality: the idea of cost changes its meaning entirely.[17]

Some economists tried to avoid this unpalatable result because it reintroduces moral problems into economics. They interpret externalities as conflicts of interest between groups which can be solved by the market system through compensation. As an example, in a case in which a factory producing vacuum cleaners fouls the air, they assume that the inhabitants of the area could raise claims for damages, "these being largely the costs of extra laundering charges and extra soap." In such cases there seems to be merely a conflict of individual interests which could be settled by making the damaging producer pay damages or install preventive devices which would increase his costs and reduce his output and the damages; or the damaged persons could pay him the same sum as a bribe to reduce his output and, thereby, their damages.[18] Mishan recommends a change in legal definition of property rights to include "amenity rights" to clean air, clear water, privacy, unspoiled nature and so forth so that the violation of such rights would entitle the victim to claim damages. However, many problems of "external" diseconomies cannot be solved by approaching them from the point of view of conflicts of individual or special group interests. This is not an entirely inappropriate approach in some cases—location of airports versus the interests of the house owners in a quiet neighborhood, noise-generating machinery in a business district; some problems of residential versus commercial or industrial zoning are of this kind. But the most glaring external "diseconomies" of today involve much more than problems of conflicts of interest. The basic problem is usually one of ethics and policy: a conflict between the profitableness of a particular good or service within the existing economic structure on the one hand,

---

[17] See also K. William Kapp, *The Social Costs of Private Enterprise* (Cambridge, Mass.: Harvard University Press, 1950).
[18] Mishan, *loc. cit.*, pp. 58–60.

and the welfare of society on the other hand. The ethical conflict is aggravated by the problem of measurement: the benefits to special interests (firms, investors, wage earners) are easily measured in terms of money profits, wages, returns; the external "disamenities" are mostly unquantifiable intangibles. The difficulty in calculating such disamenities can be seen from the efforts of certain economists who, among other devices, "add to the social cost of motorized traffic . . . by reckoning the cost of a man killed as the loss of his potential future pecuniary contribution to the national product!" [19]

Problems such as the uglification of cities, the polluting and jamming effects of motorized traffic, "the dirt and dust, the noise and smell, and the destruction and tenseness . . . but also the growing dehumanization of the physical environment . . ." are more than conflicts of interests; they are on a different level than the conflict between a noisy laundry and its neighboring residents. The "interests" of the "public at large" are not special individual or group interests: they are social goals based on moral, ethical, normative principles. Calling it an "interest," even a "long-run interest" only serves to obscure its normative character. In an oversimplified, crude but nevertheless practically valid formulation: the problem of external diseconomies involves a conflict between the acquisitive orientation in pursuit of more and more money and possessions on the one hand, and the quality of life in the present and future society on the other hand. To call them "interests" is nothing but a propagandistic trick to make these goals acceptable in a culture in which monetary and acquisitive ends reign supreme: economic aid to underdeveloped countries is "really" in the "best" interest of the United States; charity is "in reality" due to guilt feelings; humanitarian action is dressed up as the pursuit of egoistic self-interest to justify it within a utilitarian philosophy.

What is at stake in such problems as population explosion, thermonuclear destruction, biological warfare, impending starvation of millions, destruction of the environment, urban blight, over-automobilization and so forth are not only questions of social goals

---

[19] Mishan, *loc. cit.,* p. 87.

but also of *individual virtue*. Whether we want to have the short-run advantage of more roads and automobile transportation or whether we want to preserve nature and beauty for us and for our progeny involves sacrifices of immediate financial advantages under the given conditions for the sake of intangible benefits for us and for our children and grandchildren. It is a matter of moral conflict between right and wrong: whether one takes the attitude *après nous le déluge*, and pursues one's acquisitive economic interest, or whether one sacrifices now for the sake of future generations. This is a present moral problem for us, right here and now, an inner moral conflict within each living person, and not a question of individual versus social interests alone. We have become accustomed to assume that all problems can be solved by mechanical, organizational, manipulative means, in order to escape the moral dilemma. One can formulate such problems as conflicts of private versus public interests; then they become a question of organization, of a balance of power, of finding a middle ground, avoiding the necessity to choose the right and reject the wrong. Then, the moral problems can be functionalized: private firms and individuals pursue their acquisitive self-interests in terms of more money and possessions; public functionaries protect the "public interest." The inner moral conflicts are externalized, projected into the outside world and become group interests. The inner conflict within each and every individual is avoided and becomes an external conflict of interests. Is it surprising then, that the common good is transformed into the private interests of holders of political power? The consequence is corruption: they often sacrifice the public interest to their private interests because of bribery, the hope for jobs in industry and so forth. The distinction between public and private interests is obliterated.

The falsification is compounded by quantifying all "interests" and comparing them with the measuring rod of money; everything that is wrong is allowed to happen if it is only compensated by money payments. Yes, one could force the oil companies whose drilling has spoiled the magnificent Santa Barbara coastline to compensate the owners of the coastal shorelands and the people who enjoyed the clean shore and suffer from the smell; but does monetary compensation really make up for the loss of beauty and enjoyment of nature? If people have to go without these benefits, isn't this an irretrievable loss, one that cannot be replaced by money? What exists here is a *qualitative* conflict between the good, which should include a right to unspoiled nature, and monetary interests, which can only be solved by moral judgments and decisions. It is true that behind the monetary interests of corporations there may be a "public interest" in getting more oil and gasoline. In this case the conflict is between goals: either more oil, gas, cars, pollution, cementing of land, traffic jams, urban and suburban sprawl, or unspoiled open spaces and nature. Again, this conflict can only be resolved by moral judgment and decision; and such decision is not facilitated by interpreting a moral conflict in terms of a conflict between individual and group interests. The repression, elimination, avoidance of the normative dimension in social thought and philosophy has to be reversed, and social thought has to acquire again the courage for moral judgments.

SUBJECTIVISTIC CONSUMERISM

According to value-relativistic subjectivistic economic thought, individuals are supposed to maximize utility or satisfaction considered as an intangible psychic state, something obviously akin to the idea of happiness, of a pleasant, positive, inner experience. The goal of economic activity (and of life in general) is seen as a psychic state of a positive satisfying nature; but no concrete definition of this state is given, no counsel is provided on how to accomplish this state. The individual is ostensibly completely free to determine what he considers as satisfaction. Theoretically, this state of satisfaction could consist in Augustine's beatific vision and the love of God.[20] It could also be the inner state of expanded consciousness which some of modern youth and their gurus want to bring about by the use of drugs. The classical economic man was supposed to maximize something concrete: income, wealth, savings, investments, capital, durable goods, durable possessions. The

---

[20] McGill, *The Idea of Happiness*, p. 71.

value-relativistic economic man is supposed to "maximize" intangible inner psychological states and experiences. This is where economic theory reflects the changes in the temper of the times during the last hundred years in the West. It is not merely that the libertarian ideal has developed in this period—the idea that only what is held good by individuals is good in any sense; but also the idea that the individual, uninfluenced by objective reason or by any common central value system, has to decide about his own desires, goals and satisfactions. The libertarian ideal itself has changed its content: the goal of the individual shifted from building around him a concrete durable world of private property, to the idea that what matters to the individual are psychological experiences of the greatest intensity and variety. Actually the idea of maximization of individual subjective total utility contains the seed of today's frantic scramble for more and more variegated experiences, feelings, emotions, frills, kick, sensations. Value-relativistic, formalized economic reasoning was and is the first cornerstone for the building of the counterculture of the hippies, flower children, drug users, sensitivity trainers and trainees, a result which the relativistic, subjectivistic economic model builders never intended.

However, even value-relativistic economics narrows down the subjective, libertarian principle to the idea of conscious deliberate maximization and rejects the surrender to uncoordinated impulse. Such conscious maximization excludes a good many kinds of satisfaction. Maximization requires a certain permanence and stability of goals and desires in time, as indicated by the Marshallian exclusion of later "regret." Conscious deliberate maximization of satisfaction derives its pattern from technology and business and requires planning, budgeting, allocation in anticipation of future goals; then action according to plan, budget, allocation scheme, and finally reaping the reward of maximum satisfaction. The individual is mainly viewed as a consumer, and as such as a supporter of the production system. He has to show a certain stability in his behavior pattern; otherwise production could not catch up with demand. This is in conflict with completely subjective satisfaction, as illustrated by the dispute between an American economist who called "going on a binge" irrational and a European who asked "what's

irrational about going on a binge?" (1) From the point of view of
the Puritan and of the classical acquisitive economic ethic a binge
is *substantially* and *formally* irrational. It violates the moral code of
worldly asceticism and of prudent, acquisitive, productively laboring
economic man. (2) From the point of view of utilitarian economic rationality a binge is formally irrational if the planned budget of the individual concerned did not provide for this expenditure
which thus becomes irrational because it is erratic, capricious,
spontaneous and unplanned. (3) But if one abandons the limitations
imposed on economic action by the substantive ethic of Puritanism
and classicism and by the formal rationality of neoclassicism there
is no basis for calling a binge "irrational." It then receives its
"rational" character from the libertarian principle that whatever
increases individual satisfaction is positive and desirable. That this
approach was rejected by an American economist and accepted by
a European one may have to do with the unconscious remnants of
the Puritan and rationalist tradition in the United States and its
destruction in Europe. Be this as it may, the individualistically libertarian principle, unqualified by any substantial moral directives
about what is right or wrong, unrestricted even by the postulate of
conscious deliberate choice based on a planned budget and maximization over time, does not yield any guidelines for action at all.
It simply implies that the individual does what he does at any given
moment and calls it maximization of satisfaction or utility. Maximization or simply satisfaction becomes an empty word duplicating
behavior, a fictitious "force" or "motive" assumed to lurk behind
any kind of behavior. This approach deprives individual behavior
of any traces of economic rationality in the utilitarian or neoclassical sense. A person may have made a budget, allocating $50 to
pay his college tuition; then an impulse overcomes him and he
spends it instead on the proverbial "binge." The next day he has a
hangover, and regrets his deviation from the budget. According to
interpretation (3) this is still "maximization of satisfaction or
utility" and, therefore, not necessarily irrational.

This model of behavior certainly underlies modern advertising which aims at seducing buyers into "binges" of spending. The
modern consumer is not supposed to be a rational economic "man"

who shops with a predetermined plan and knows precisely what he wants; but rather an "irrational woman" who, in order to kill time, enters a department store and, lured by the titillating seduction of the exhibited treasures, spends money on impulse and for "kicks." Advertising psychology fits in precisely with the disintegration of economic rationality from a substantive idea to a content-empty subjectivistic scheme. In view of the fact that the Western economies require continuous "spending binges" by consumers, it is important to understand that this "irrational" economic behavior depends on an intellectual scheme which views the economy from an individualistic point of view and individual behavior as directed toward the intensification and variegation of subjective experiences. This intellectual scheme, however, implicitly justifies the excesses of the drug- and counterculture; they differ from the "binges" induced by advertising only by their rebellious motivation.

A binge *can* be considered as rational behavior; only we are confronted here with a kind of rationality different from the rationality of utilitarian, neoclassical and even of value-relativistic economic man. Robbins defines as "irrational" the surrender to "the blind force of external stimuli and unco-ordinated impulse at every moment." [21] This is exactly what the "binge" is. There is, however, a new and different "rationality" that has emerged in the youth and radical movements of today. The way for this new "rationality" has been prepared by the idea widely held by psychologists of the psychoanalytic and similar persuasions that repression, the holding in of impulses, is mentally and physically unhealthy. Living and acting out such impulses can be considered as a new ethic, rooted in ideas about the nature of men, the psyche, the balance of inner forces. Some psychologists recommend a "binge" as an occasional "outlet" for pent-up drives and longings (like keeping a second set of dishes ready to be smashed on the concrete of the patio as an outlet for anger which otherwise might be directed against wife and children). This behavior, irrational in the light of all concepts of economic man (Puritan, classical, neo-

---

[21] Robbins, *Essay on the Nature and Significance of Economic Science,* p. 157.

classical, utilitarian and Robbins-ian) becomes "rational" in the light of a new image of man.

The new (psychological) image of man presents him as a system composed of many dimensions, factors, forces, drives, longings, aspirations. The system is one of countervailing forces kept in a precarious balance by the ego, continuously pressured by reality, the superego and the unconscious id. As such it serves as a prototype of the image from which the new kind of rationality is derived. The ego acts like the managers of large corporations or like officials of the Federal Government, trying to arrive at a compromise between various pressure groups. Its rationality consists in providing safety valves for overwhelming pressures and for supporting countervailing pressures. (This analogy may be more than a simile. Both types of rationality—the economic and the psychological one —are derived from technical and socioeconomic prototypes which reflect social conditions: the economic one from the machine and the older profit maximizing business firm; the psychological image from the modern corporation managers and the way modern governments function. In both cases the images of individual man and of society show similar traits. They are interrelated and reenforce each other.)

The conflict between "rationality" and "irrationality" in industrial society reveals itself as a conflict between two types of rationality, economic and psychological. The structure of traditional economic thought and the image of the economy it presents become untenable when psychological rationality replaces economic rationality. Without stable, enduring goals which can be measured, compared and maximized, no individual equilibrium is possible on which a social one could rest. The stable, equilibrated economic universe breaks down if people become more and more inclined to go on "binges." This is why the hippies, the flower children, the rebel fringe groups generate such hostility and anxiety. They destroy the ethos of economic rationalism. This development has been prepared by and, at the same time, is reflected in the intellectual approaches and constructs of economists and psychologists. The moment individual subjective need satisfaction is introduced as the main normative principle there is no reason why the conscious maximizing rationality of old-fashioned economic man should remain a supreme value. Elevating "the binge" to the supreme goal if and when individual drives require a living out of impulses became a logical step facilitated by the individualistic, subjective libertarian principle. Once rationality is empty of content, denuded of any idea of "restrictive" virtues, living out one's impulses becomes as rational as "maximization of utility."

However, the model of economic man developed by value-relativistic economics does not consistently apply its value-empty subjectivistic principle. It is not really completely empty of substantial objective values; it is related to specific economic institutions. It implies maximization of acquisition in terms of money, and in terms of the goods and services money can buy in the modern economy. Few economists would want to legitimize any "binge." They think in terms of utilities yielded by goods bought and subject to the "measuring rod of money." All maximization-of-utility models imply acquisitive maximization, getting more and more goods whose utility can be measured by a common quantitative denominator, such as money. Even if it were logically possible to apply such a "maximization" model to the medieval, monastic ideals of poverty, chastity and obedience, I have grave doubts that economists had such a case in mind. The Benedictine monks were among the first who applied rational discipline to economic activity; but they did not aim at maximization of products or utility but at a target income sufficient for their support so that they could exercise the Christian virtues. The maximization model is not geared to such a situation, although one could imagine some logistical acrobatics that would make it applicable. What has happened to the ideal of economic man can be compared to a picture stolen from a museum, leaving only the frame. The picture was of acquisitive economic man. Subjectivistic value theory transformed the goal of acquisition into the living out of impulses; this removed the picture: only the frame of formal "maximization" remains; an ascetic monk or a member of a hippie commune would look very strange in the same frame.

The formalization and subjectivization of economic rationality also opened the way for the *consumerism* of our days: the un-restricted pursuit of "pleasure" through the acquisition and the use of an ever-increasing volume and variety of goods and services. As long as vestiges of the Puritan ethic with its impulse control, its injunction to save and practice prudent consumption habits was amalgamated with economic rationalism, the bourgeois orientation toward consumption was ambivalent. Consumption had to be justified by morally approved purposes: survival, reproducing the race, keeping fit, wholesomeness, durability of the environment, enlargement of the personality, the creativity of work itself, the satisfaction of an instinct of workmanship. The demotion of en-compassing to technical reason removed any basis for such restric-tions on consumption. Consumption changed from a relation of the individual to his property which was experienced by him as an enlargement of his personality, to wallowing in sensual experiences which required that goods and services be swallowed up, digested and discarded, so that the consumption process could start over again. The old type of consumption corresponding to the Puritan ethos and the value orientation of classical and neoclassical econ-omics was related to work and aimed at the acquisition of durable goods. Work creates durable goods which become durable property. The end of production and consumption was then the creation of an artificial durable world, composed of private property, as an ex-tension and support of the individual personality.[22] The modern consumerism for which formalism and value-relativism opened the way, is related to labor and to the metabolic process.[23]

Consumption of the fantastic volume and variety of goods and services produced by the present Western economies becomes a never-ending, always increasing metabolic process. Albert Moravia has compared the modern consumer to a "gut" which, like very simple organisms that have only mouth, intestines and anus, does nothing but ingest, digest and discharge, an intestinal tube which,

[22] H. Arendt, *The Human Condition:* "Work provides an artificial world of things. Within its borders each individual life is housed while this world itself is meant to outlast and transcend them all."

[23] "Labor is the activity which corresponds to the biological process of the human body" to its "spontaneous growth, metabolism and eventual decay." Arendt, *loc. cit.,* p. 7.

in the end, produces nothing but excrement. All modern consumer goods are "ingested, digested and discharged in an immense quantity . . ." [24] It is the elimination of the normative content from economic rationality which made this metabolical consumerism of modern man possible because it destroyed any rational basis for moral restraint in consumption and production. This change was reflected in economic theory by the distinction between the old-fashioned "rational" consumer and the new "irrational consumer" influenced by advertising which represents the intrusion of "psychological rationality" into economics. The old type of "purely rational" consumer (the consumer under pure competition) chose between homogeneous, standardized products merely on a price basis; he acted like a "rational" economic man, buying as cheaply as possible. He has no preferences for the products of different sellers, except for their cheaper price or better quality. A commodity is to him something unequivocal, a thing with a definite objective quality, defined and circumscribed by physical characteristics and clearly delimited from other goods.

The modern consumer developed a psychological attitude toward goods which makes possible advertising and selling methods, "product differentiation" in modern economic parlance. This consumer does not see a commodity as a definite physical object. He has a feeling for the nuances and differences of products, caused by the "conditions surrounding its sale." The retail buyer considers brand names, packaging, styling; he considers "the seller's location, the general tone of character of his establishment, his way of doing business, his reputation for fair dealing, courtesy, efficiency, and all personal links which attach him either to the seller himself or those employed by him" [25] ; all these "intangible" elements become part of the "products," differentiating similar physical goods from each other in the minds of the consumers. The consumer has become interested in things which previously may have been considered as accidental and extraneous.

---

[24] Albert Moravia, *The Red Book and the Great Wall,* trans. by Ronald Horn (New York: Farrar, Straus & Giroux, 1968), pp. 13 ff.
[25] Edward Chamberlin, *The Theory of Monopolistic Competition* (Cambridge, Mass.: Harvard University Press, 1933), pp. 56 ff.

Economics has always considered economic processes to involve the interrelations between abstract objects like commodities, money, and so forth. Product differentiation has been made amenable to discussion by disguising it in a redefinition of the concepts of commodity and industry. What was discovered here was a new psychological attitude on the part of consumers, a new type of motivation for economic behavior. The attitude of consumers that makes "product differentiation" possible has probably developed since the beginning of the twentieth century. (I would like to leave open the question whether this attitude truly represents a twentieth-century development, or whether it has existed all along and was overlooked by economic theory because it did not conform to its "rationalist" interpretations.) The history of effective advertising requires a correspondingly receptive attitude on the part of consumers. Not until the 1930's did economic theory begin to acknowledge this type of motivation. The fact that consumers may prefer to pay a higher price because they are attracted by the color of the package or the looks of the salesgirl does not fit into the picture of "economic man." The final recognition and admission that consumers act, not only on the basis of purely economic advantage but also motivated by a host of capricious, impulsive, spontaneous, emotional and habitual factors represents the introduction of a new "irrational" element into economic analysis; "irrational" only because it deviates from the traditional conceptual frame but rational from the psychological point of view.

This irrationality in consumption is the consequence not only of affluence but of formalistic utility and welfare theory which push the individual in the direction of value-emptiness by removing any traces of the objective right and the common good. When the individual is not harnessed to the guide of a conscience, he can accept any fashionable attitude that is promulgated by advertising and adopted by the peer group. There is much revulsion against the bizarre and abstruse styles in life and art adopted by the leftist and deviant counterculture. What is overlooked, however, is that these trends were prepared by the subjectivistic value-emptiness of the consumers' market manipulated by profit-seeking sellers. If people are supposed to be free to fall for senseless consumers' goods, there is nothing to prevent them from being hippies, yippies, etc. The difference between the excesses of the Western *haute* and *basse couture* and the *épater le bourgeois* dress of the hippies and young- sters is very small indeed. The life-style of the deviants is digested so fast by the advertising media that yesterday's protest becomes today's fashion.

Modern consumerism is a dialectical phenomenon. It is partly caused by the structure of the modern Western economy which requires ever more spending and consumption for economic growth. It is also a result of the breakdown of impulse-control and of the decline of the bourgeois value system. It is interrelated with certain trends in Neo-Freudian social utopianism. In a way West- ern consumerism is an extension of the pleasure principle into the economic sphere—a pleasure principle liberated from the ascetic restrictions of the Puritan and nineteenth-century bourgeois ethos. One can compare this process of gradual liberation in the con- sumption sphere with a similar process in the sexual sphere. Eco- nomic attitudes toward consumption began with the prohibition and restriction of superfluous and luxurious consumption by the Puritan ethos. This was continued in classical economics by the prohibition of prodigal spending and consumption; and by the re- striction of consumption to moderate, prudent expenditure, aiming at the acquisition of durable, lasting goods. Finally, this develop- ment resulted in the breaking down of all restrictions to allow, even to enjoin, unlimited spending for unrestricted sensual experi- ence and pleasure. This development is paralleled in the sexual sphere: first restriction of sexuality to monogamous heterosexual- ity in marriage; then loosening of sexual mores to allow more and more extramarital heterosexual intercourse; until, in recent times, almost everything goes: group sex, wife swapping, pornog- raphy, perversions, and so forth, corresponding to the consumption orgies of the modern economy.

In modern advertising consumerist and sexual liberation are combined. Modern consumerism is accompanied by an erotization of life in general, apart from strictly sexual activity. The increasing use of sexual stimulation in advertising shows clearly the combina- tion of eroticism with selling, spending and consumption. This is not merely a selling technique; it represents a tendency of the times toward diffusion of sexuality. From its heterosexual, monogamous form sexuality expanded gradually to encompass and permeate extrasexual spheres of life. Sexuality today is intermixed with the spending of money and the acquisition of goods. This is more than the Freudian idea that money earning and spending can be traced back to libidinous drives which may have been true even in Victorian times when advertising was in its infancy. What takes place today is a conscious erotization of consumption. Psychoanalysis maintains that the child sexualizes everything; true or not, modern selling certainly does sexualize consumers' spending. This is sexuality separated from the human object, and diffused, diluted with buying and with goods. The spirit of modern advertising reflects clearly the trend of modern ideologies about sex and eros. Relations between economics and eros are probably ubiquitous phenomena: the work and success ethos was combined with restrictive, monogamous heterosexuality; the modern mass consumption society with the diffusion of sex into spending and consumption.

Consumerism is also related to the change in sex roles. In nineteenth-century Victorian society spending was a female function. The man earned the income, the woman disbursed it. The embellishment of life, aesthetic pursuits, entertainment, leisure were the province of women. In a way, the growing importance of spending, entertainment, comforts, leisure and consumption can be regarded as part of a social trend toward the feminization of men and of society. In a patriarchal society women and everything they stood for were repressed. In modern consumerism, with its stress on erotization, sensuality, sensations, the repressed female element is liberated and widely accepted by both men and women; they both have become interested in those sensual and emotional experiences which are inseparable from modern spending and consumption. Consumerism is part of the process of "feminization" in the sense that both men and women in the economy of mass consumption have to have the tastes and lead the kind of life that was considered feminine in nineteenth-century Western society.

5

Market Power, Managerialism
and the Reintroduction of Values

It is significant for the style of modern social thought that the
debate about the free market was mostly conducted in terms of
external economic institutions and seldom in terms of moral philosophy, of right and wrong. The entire discussion about the free
market versus governmental planning is centered around the distinction between private individuals and firms operating in a free
market versus governmental agencies planning for the entire
economy. As important as this distinction is economically, socially
and politically and as large as it looms in popular propaganda, it
overlooks the question of goals, ends, priorities, the basic moral
questions involved in economic action. The problem is not merely
who should make the decisions in the economy—private individuals
and firms or governmental agencies—but *what* decisions are, will
and should be made. The question of *what* is neglected in favor of
the question of *who* should be the decision makers. This is due to
the heritage of the free market philosophy in its value-empty form.
We have become so accustomed to assume that a free, suprapersonal
market will coordinate random individual decisions and actions and

channel them into the right direction that we concentrate only on the mechanism of allocation but not on its content and results. The free market philosophy has contributed its fair share to the destruction of social and individual morality.

This, however, began to change with the decline of the free market and its philosophy, under the impact of the following events:

1. The growth of big business, monopolies, market power, cartels, and so forth in the Western economies and the countervailing growth of governmental control and unionism.

2. The disruption of the free market system through World War I, the subsequent abandonment of the gold standard, growing protectionism, the manipulation of monetary systems and of domestic markets through central banking, tariffs, subsidies, regulations, and so forth.

3. The Great Depression of the 1930's which undermined the belief in the automatic, self-regenerating powers and beneficiality of the free market. It gave a powerful impetus to the trend toward political interference with and manipulation of the economy during and after the Roosevelt Administration.

These events led to the disintegration, not of the free enterprise system as we understand it today (as distinct from socialism and communism) but of the nineteenth-century free market ideology. The belief in the invisible hand of the competitive market was gradually abandoned and replaced by the recognition that the visible hand of corporate private and public organizations and of their managers allocate resources and determine our economic fate. Conscious, deliberate, corporate managerial economic decision-making gradually entered the universe of discourse of economists. Conscious decisions imply, as said before, relatively free choices between alternatives and require normative (ethical, moral, political) guiding principles for such choices. Inevitably, the normative, repressed and neglected by the free market ideology, reentered the scene. This raised various problems: (1) How does the (limited) freedom of corporations with monopoly and market power affect the alleged theoretical certainty of economic theory and its ability to predict the movements of prices and the processes of the market? (2) What motivations and goals determine the choices and decisions of corporate managers? In the history of economic thought these questions were discussed mostly in relation to the market power of big business.

MARKET POWER AND CERTAINTY [1]

The free market ideology excludes and denies the existence of market power. By definition a market is free only if no firm can influence the prices of the things it buys or sells by its own individual actions. Market prices and their changes are determined by the interrelation of supply and demand, by supraindividual market forces which are supposed to be the unintended by-product of the decisions of many individuals pursuing their own self-interest. The single firm can sell at the market price or refrain from selling; but it cannot influence this price. This situation was called "perfect" or "pure" competition and was represented on a two-dimensional diagram (where the vertical axis represents the price and the horizontal axis the quantity that can be sold) by a "horizontal demand curve." This simply means that the firm has to sell at the market price but would not find a buyer if it asked for a higher price because there are many competitors who are willing to sell at the (lower) market price. In such a free market the individual firm (the small independent businessman or farmer) has little free choice and can only accept the market price. If he cannot make a profit at this price, he has to leave the market or go bankrupt. He is nothing but a small pebble crushed by the steamroller of the competitive market. He must adjust or fall by the wayside; but because he has no choice, he also has no moral problems, no problems of goals, ends, values except profit maximization. The competitive free market makes the choice for him and leads his profit-seeking activities, through the famous invisible hand, into the direction of what is assumed to be the common good: ever-increasing production in accordance with consumer demand.

---

[1] The theoretical discussion of market power that began in the 1930's was conducted in technical terms, with the help of what has been called the "box of tools" (marginal analysis, trigonometry, and geometrical and mathematical models). Therefore, the use of some technical jargon is inevitable in this section.

However, with the growing importance of large-scale business and the growing visibility of its power, the blinders of economic theory were removed, although slowly. Not before the 1930's was the free market model modified by the concept of *imperfect competition.*[2] The existence of monopoly power was admitted as an important feature in many markets in the form of a geometrical "gadget" of a declining (instead of a horizontal) demand curve. This simply means that a firm which has some market power will not lose all of its customers if it charges a higher price than its competitors. It will perhaps lose some sales but not all of them. This market power will usually be based on a relatively large share of the market: General Motors would certainly not lose *all* of its sales if it charged somewhat higher prices than Ford and Chrysler. Ford and Chrysler could not expand their production sufficiently to replace GM's output, thus, too many people would have to go without a car. So people will buy GM cars, even at higher prices, instead of going without an automobile; although the higher prices may reduce GM's sales, they will not fall to zero. This is the meaning of a declining (instead of a horizontal) demand curve.

With a declining demand curve the firm has, theoretically, a choice between selling more at a lower price and less at a higher price, between making more or less profits, or between profits and other goals. The technical meaning aside, this means that *there is a choice,* and choice requires decisions based on normative rules, principles, goals, even "ideals." Thus, at least a limited sphere of freedom from the inescapable supraindividual market forces seems to have been opened. The firm with market power (with a declining demand curve) is in a position to forgo maximum short-run profits for other goals such as smaller but stable long-run profits, stability of operations, undisturbed relations with customers, suppliers, labor force and so forth. Such firms may actually be influenced by moral considerations about the common good, the welfare of its employees, the aesthetics of installations. In a way, the acknowledgment of the existence of market power

---

[2] Joan Robinson, *The Economics of Imperfect Competition* (London: Macmillan, 1950).

(through the introduction of the declining demand curve) represents the first break with the laissez-faire philosophy in traditional economic thought. Through a geometrical device, the possibility of choice, decisions and alternative goals was admitted.

This admission, however, was considered to be incompatible with attainment of the "scientific" precision and certainty to which economists have aspired ever since Ricardo. Economics has always pretended to be what today is called a "hard science," assumed to require firm, unequivocal laws and precise predictions of the future. Such claims were supposed to be met by what is called equilibrium theory. It was—and still is—assumed that in a free market economy the supraindividual forces will move prices, costs and profits toward an equilibrium level; this means a situation in which no changes in prices and quantities supplied and demanded will and can be brought about by any firm in the market because each of them has reached a position in which it makes the largest possible profits. In this case the firms who are actually producing and selling in the market are in equilibrium because they are making the largest profits possible under the given conditions (as to costs, prices, demand for the product and the number of competitors). The market itself is in equilibrium because, at the prevailing price, the quantities supplied and demanded are equal and because other firms are not able or willing to sell at this price and not able or willing to underbid the firms in the market and to drive down the price. Price theory assumes that such equilibria are predictable; supraindividual market forces lead to what has been called a "determinate" equilibrium solution.

It is not our purpose here to enter a thorough critique of this approach. It is sufficient to understand that the certainty of the "determinate" equilibrium solution is largely fictitious and that equilibrium analysis cannot be the basis of predictions. The statement that, if there is an excess of supply over demand at a certain relatively high price (for example, of coffee in Brazil), the price will fall until demand and supply become equal is not a prediction but an economic "law" that will "work" under certain conditions. Equilibrium is an "iffy" proposition: it will be reached *if* certain conditions are present. Whether they are or will be present can only be established by empirical investigation which is usually in-conclusive. The precision and certainty of theoretical equilibrium models are mostly a self-deception of economic theorists.

Some have maintained that a difference exists in respect to de-terminateness and predictability between a competitive laissez-faire market and a market with market power (oligopoly: a few large firms, as in the production of automobiles). The former is allegedly determinate and predictable, the latter indeterminate and unpre-dictable. The fact is that both can be indeterminate and unpre-dictable. The events in the real world, in the actual economy as it was and is, have never been precisely foreseeable and predictable. When the laissez-faire economists talk about predictable determin-ateness, they are making hypothetical statements: *If* there is a rela-tively large number of independent buyers and sellers, *if* future demand and supply are known to them, *if* the buyers and sellers are able and willing to engage in price competition (outbid and underbid each other), *if* their intentions (demand and supply) do not change, *then* the price will move into the direction of an equi-librium price at which quantities demanded and quantities supplied are equal. This scheme is not a prediction unless we know for sure that all the "ifs" are present in reality; these "ifs" require that all participants in the market know each other's intentions; such knowledge does not exist, except perhaps in organized markets such as stock exchanges, or in markets where all buyers and sellers are present. This in itself, however, would not necessarily prevent economics from being a "hard" science. The situation would not be different from physics: a physicist can precisely formulate the law of gravity but cannot precisely predict how fast a specific rock will fall in the atmosphere. The "softness" of economics lies in the factors which the equilibrium models leave out of consideration: that firms and individuals can pursue innumerable goals outside of profit maximization. It is important to understand that the tradi-tional equilibrium model of the free market leaves out the limited sphere of freedom of action which human beings have under any conditions. This limited freedom was rediscovered in the form of the declining demand curve and interpreted as a result of market power. However, limited freedom of action exists also without market power. Even in a free market firms could forgo part of their normal profits and refrain from profit *maximization*, that is, be satisfied with profits lower than they *could* make. They could do this for noneconomic motives, for example, to alleviate poverty by selling at lower prices to people in need. That this would not fit in with the attitudes required by the free market system does not eliminate the possibilities of, at least occasionally, abandoning those attitudes; the freedom to do so is always given, regardless of the presence or absence of market power.

This, however, economic theory cannot admit for two reasons: (1) it would destroy the alleged certainty and determinateness of its predictions; (2) it would admit that economic action may be influenced by noneconomic motives: that profit maximization is not the only possible goal even in the economic field. If firms can pursue various goals in addition to profit maximization, then the market processes become "indeterminate"; not only concretely unpredictable (which they are anyway) but they cannot even be theoretically represented as an equilibrium situation in terms of profit maximization. Then the entire theoretical structure of the free market model would break down. Furthermore, if the single firm can deviate from the goal of profit maximization, the acquisitive attitude, the ethos of more and more is implicitly put into doubt. The rediscovery of even a limited freedom from profit maximization puts in doubt the theoretical and moral structure of the "free enterprise system."

Therefore, imperfect competition theory was quick to block the avenue of freedom opened up by the declining demand curve by assuming that the firm would still, in spite of its freedom of choice, maximize profits; this precluded any choice. The firm would have to produce an output which would guarantee maximum profits (technically: the output at which marginal cost would be equal to marginal revenue). In spite of opening the way for choices (symbolized by the declining demand curve), the theory closed the possibility of choice again by postulating that the firm would not choose any other goal but profit maximization. The admission of freedom of choice and thereby of the application of moral and normative principles to business decisions was like opening a door slightly only to close it again by the assumption that profit maximization was the only possible goal.

In order to demonstrate that the basic laissez-faire philosophy and its theoretical structure were not impaired by the discovery of declining demand curves and market power, the new theory was called "imperfect competition," indicating that the basic value-attitude was still the ideology of free competition. The situation of the firm under imperfect competition was compared unfavorably with the purely competitive one: higher prices and lower output were seen as the detrimental consequences of imperfect competition. It was assumed that the imperfection of competition prevented the optimum allocation of resources which the free market (pure competition) would have brought about. However, although the free market was still the ideal, the recognition of imperfections was a first step toward the decline of the libertarian ideology.

The same stance was taken in monopolistic competition theory.[3] Again the attempt was made to save the idea of free competition; but the obstacles to pure free market competition were now called "monopolistic" to indicate that monopoly or market power was the root of its "imperfections." Attention was devoted to the importance of oligopoly. This approach led to the recognition of another factor, beyond the declining demand curve, which disturbed the determinateness of the equilibrium theory of the market. It was discovered that the demand curve itself was not a given, objectively determinable fact but a variable factor which large-scale firms can manipulate through intensive advertising. This is what Galbraith later called the dependence effect and the creation of demand by the large producer and supplier (in *The Affluent Society* and in *The New Industrial State*). The idea that prices and quantities produced move toward a predictable, definable (determinate) equilibrium position rested on the assumption that firms can know their demand, that is, know what quantities they can sell at various prices. This requires that demand should be a known objective fact (a parameter) independent of the actions of

---

[3] Chamberlin, *The Theory of Monopolistic Competition.*

any individual firm in the market. In markets with a few large firms this is not the case. Each large firm can manipulate its own demand which becomes a variable, dependent on the firm's action for two reasons: first, the firm's decisions and actions in respect to price, output, styling, advertising, and so forth have an effect on the competitors. They will react to these decisions in some indefinite, unpredictable way. These reactions, in turn, will influence the demand curve of the firm that started the chain reaction. In this way, the firm's decisions and actions indirectly influence its own demand curve. Second, the oligopolistic firm can manipulate its own demand curve by advertising and other methods of "product differentiation" such as trademarks and brand names. The firm can persuade the consumer to buy its products even at a somewhat higher price (within certain price ranges) and thereby increase its own freedom of choice in regard to price, output, quality, styling and other policies.

In no sense of the word can the demand curve then be considered to be a "given" fact (parameter). Any assumption of a definite, determinate equilibrium, to be defined in terms of a definite relation between output, cost and revenue became now impossible. The equilibrium of the firm and of the market became now wholly "indeterminate." [4]

This statement has important philosophical implications for the value attitude of modern capitalism. It raises the problem of choice and the problem of values which were obliterated under the impact of a laissez-faire philosophy. The new situation must lead to a different model of economic behavior. Whereas it is assumed that the individual entrepreneur in a completely free market (under pure competition) must maximize profits (equalize marginal cost and price) if he does not want to fall by the wayside economically, the large-scale firm could—if its managers wanted to—pursue all sorts of other goals. Under the purely competitive system the firm supposedly had to act "rationally" by maximizing profits; under large-scale, corporate, oligopoly capitalism the firm can pursue goals which may be considered economically "irra-

---

[4] Robert Triffin, *Monopolistic Competition and General Equilibrium Theory* (Cambridge, Mass.: Harvard University Press, 1940).

tional" from the point of view of classical and neoclassical economic philosophy. This obviously opens the door for a reexamination of the goals of the firm and of the economy which was closed by traditional economic thinking.

Ultimately we are confronted here with two different world images. The model of pure competition reflects the world image of classical Newtonian physics and its underlying philosophy. There the object of observation and the analyzing observer are completely separated. The world is like a clock which runs independently from the observer ruled by absolute time, absolute space, an absolute substance of mass, and unequivocal causality. The world is like a planetarium—atomistic, mechanistic; thought and observation merely reflect this universe like a mirror image. This is also the world image of classical and neoclassical economics and of laissez-faire economics (pure competition). Here, the individual (buyer, seller, consumer, worker) has the same position as the observer in the Newtonian world image; he is subject to the laws which he can only observe but cannot influence; he can only adjust and submit to them. The individual firm and consumer in a laissez-faire economy must try to do the same as the observer in classical physics: try to grasp the objective "real" facts and adjust his own plans and aspirations to them. At best, he can aspire to predict correctly but never to control the economic universe.

This world image changed with the advent of the relativity theory and quantum physics and the discovery of the Heisenberg principle.[5] The characteristic of this new world outlook is that the course of an event is not always independent of the observer. No clear dividing line exists between the measuring apparatus of the observer and the object under consideration; reality is a combination of both the observer and his actions and the observed object. In Heisenberg's words: "Man now only confronts himself. The object of research is not any more nature as such but nature as exposed to human questioning. Research focuses on the network of the relations between man and nature" (*Das Weltbild der Physik*). Or as Andrade has expressed it: "observation disturbs

---

[5] See also Kenneth E. Boulding, "Economics as a Moral Science," *American Economic Review*, vol. LXXVIII, no. 2 (February, 1969), 1 ff.

reality." [6] The image of the market as presented in oligopoly and monopolistic competition theory resembles this situation. It asserts that one cannot arrive at determinate, precise "predictions" because the outcome of every move depends on relatively free decisions of a small group of firms with market power. Because they are not completely subject to market forces, they have a range of choice. This range of freedom not only makes it impossible to predict what they will do, but, because of their market power, they will change the very conditions in the market on which all predictions would have to be based. The reaction of other firms to such changes in the market is equally uncertain; they too have a range of choice and freedom, and, again, these reactions will change market conditions. In a laissez-faire economy which conforms to the purely competitive model, the individual supposedly has no range of choice. His hand is forced by the conditions of the market. There, economic forces are like an avalanche which carries every individual with it, *nolens volens*. Under oligopoly the large firms have a number of choices as to how to act and how to react to the action of others. All this will change the market conditions which, in turn, makes prediction impossible.

In markets with a few, large, powerful firms, demand, supply of labor, materials, and so forth are not facts with which the firm is inevitably confronted but they can be planned and determined by the firm. The economic reality becomes then a combination of unalterable facts on the one hand, and conditions which can be influenced by the firms on the other hand. In economic reality the corporate (and the public) manager "encounters himself," or finds what he has created, a situation similar to the Heisenberg principle. Thus, economic reality becomes the result of managerial action. Technically, what used to be parameters in action became variables which action can determine, change, influence. The most obvious example is demand: under laissez-faire it confronts the seller as an unalterable fact; with market power a large producer can create it and change it by advertising. The indeterminacy results from the fact that more and more parameters become variables, because

---

[6] Quoted from F. W. Matson, *The Broken Image* (New York: George Braziller, 1964), p. 143.

they can be influenced by the large firms. This approach shows obvious parallels to Heisenberg's indeterminateness. In both cases it is the observer (in physics) or the actor-manager (the firm with market power), that is, the individual involved, which causes indeterminateness; that the individual is the observer in one case and the actor in the other does not change the similarity. In Heisenberg's interpretation, observation becomes action because it changes reality like action. In the case of the large firm, the actor-manager changes reality which he then "observes" in its changed aspects. In the new concept of reality, observer and actor become one and perform a similar role; they change reality. This is in line with the tendency of the modern age which reversed the roles of knowledge and action. Technology applied in industry led to a situation in which certainty of knowledge could only be reached under the condition that "knowledge concerned only what one had done himself . . ." [7] Thinking becomes making and doing, and reality becomes what man has made. In quantum physics the nature of reality becomes uncertain and dependent on the method of observation: the ultimate nature of matter could either be particles or waves, according to the method used. The image of reality is thus changed from an objective one, independent of the observer and actor, from a "genuine photographic reproduction of an independent reality out there," to a "subjective creation of the mind" and of action.

There is an intriguing dialectical conflict hidden in this situation. In both physics and economics the older classical image of reality is supposed to lead to determinate, certain, unambiguous, precise laws, whereas the new relativistic, subject-object combining image leads to uncertainty and indeterminateness. The certainty of the classical economic system is derived from the powerlessness and lack of freedom of the individual firms. The uncertainty of the markets with large firms is derived from their market power. However, H. Arendt explains the substitution of doing and making for contemplation and thought by the *quest for certainty* of knowledge. Market power and monopoly have also been

---

[7] H. Arendt, *The Human Condition*, p. 290.

explained by the quest for security and certainty. Firms, especially those with large investment, try to assure the safety and profitability of this investment by monopolistic practices.[8] Galbraith explains the policies of large corporations by the necessity of making sure of demand and of the supply of the means of production in order to secure stability, growth and returns. Equally, government manipulation of the economy has been justified as a means to remove future uncertainty.[9] In the view of critics of the market system it is the "anarchy" of the market, that is, its uncertainty, instability, its indeterminateness, which requires remedy through socialist planning.

Thus, we find here an inconsistency. On the one hand the competitive, free, laissez-faire market seems to lead to *determinate*, certain principles, laws, predictions, whereas the economy administered by corporate and public managers leads to indeterminacy, that is uncertainty. On the other hand the free market is considered to be uncertain and unpredictable, and the managed economy predictable. This conflict is a dialectical one: it cannot be solved by stating that one or the other approach is right or wrong. What underlies this antinomy is an ideological conflict: seen from the point of view of the laissez-faire philosophy and the model of pure competition, the result of market forces seems predictable and unequivocally determined. Their result is also implicitly considered to be "good" and beneficial for the individual and society. From this point of view the interference of public and corporate managers disturbs the harmony of the market and leads to uncertainty and indeterminacy. It is paradoxical that the image of the beneficial free market designed by laissez-faire theory—supposedly a system of economic liberty—does not leave the individual any freedom. He can adjust to the market or go bankrupt. His range of freedom is much smaller than that of the managers of large corporations. Laissez-faire economic philosophy leads to a rigidly deterministic image of the economy in which inexorable economic laws force buyers and sellers into submission; this is

---

[8] J. A. Schumpeter, *Capitalism, Socialism and Democracy* (New York: Harper & Row, 1950), pp. 87 ff.

[9] A. Loewe, *On Economic Knowledge* (New York: Harper & Row, 1965).

what makes the end result seem certain and predictable. Economic freedom is restricted here by the laws of the market.

The oligopolistic market composed of large firms seems to grant much greater freedom to those firms, thereby making the outcome uncertain and indeterminate. The market power which, to the laissez-faire economist, is the enemy of freedom, makes the economy indeterminate because of the higher degree of freedom it seems to grant to large producers and sellers. The economic freedom of others, however, is restricted by this market power.

We have shown that in theory even the freedom of the large firms has been taken away again by the assumption of profit maximization as the only possible goal of even the large firm. In this way the indeterminateness is removed. The firm will produce the profit-maximizing output and forgo the possibility of choosing between this and other goals. Market power has again been caught in the net of deterministic theory and the disturbing freedom of choice is eliminated by the assumption of a singular goal: profit maximization. The unity of the traditional theoretical framework and its determinateness is preserved by a *normative* postulate: that the managers of the firm will choose only to maximize profits and nothing else. The unity of the old laissez-faire, and of the new monopolistic competition theory is preserved by the utilitarian acquisitive morality which is supposed to motivate all business behavior in the old competitive and in the new capitalist economy with market power. As long as firms aim at profit maximization, the outcome will be determinate and predictable, whether these firms are large or small, with or without market power.

The crucial element in this picture is a basic moral conflict about goals. As long as profit maximization is assumed as the goal, unity, determinacy and predictability are maintained. As soon as this assumption is abandoned, and other goals besides profit maximization are admitted, indeterminacy arises and the entire theoretical framework begins to crumble. And it should be well understood that the assumption of profit maximization is not a purely intellectual and scientific problem, not merely and not predominantly a true or false question, but a normative moral question: should or should we not, as managers, consumers, workers, savers, investors, spenders aim exclusively at more and more money or are there other goals worthy of considerations? Traditional economic theory tried to preserve its constructs by preserving the profit motive and the acquisitive attitude. In the following we shall trace their further demise and show that they have ceased to be the chief basis of economic thought.

MANAGERIALISM AND REPRESENTATION

The element of market power of large firms in the United States became, in the last quarter of the nineteenth century, a political problem. The first antitrust law, the Sherman Act of 1890, bears testimony to this. However, as we have seen, it took nearly half a century before this fact penetrated economic theory, a process accompanied and reenforced by institutional and statistical studies of the concentration of economic power and the decline of price competition in the classical and neoclassical sense.[10] A. A. Berle and G. C. Means [11] showed conclusively how the idea of private property was changed by the separation of management and ownership in the modern, large-scale corporation. Their influential work was highly critical of the loss of power by owners (stockholders) and of the subsequent decline of the profit motive in our economy. They argued that the profit motive can work as an incentive only in an economy in which those who make business decisions have to bear the consequences of their decisions. This requires that the same individuals bear the risks and manage the enterprise (a combination of management and ownership in the same hands) or, in corporations, a tight control of management by the stockholders. Berle and Means have written the history of the disintegration of this control and described the emergence of management as a relatively independent group, "a self-perpetuating oligarchy" not responsible to anybody and hardly restricted by any competition. A. R. Burns wrote a history of the disintegration

---

[10] J. K. Galbraith, "Monopoly and the Concentration of Economic Power," in H. S. Ellis (ed.), *A Survey of Contemporary Economics* (Philadelphia: Blakiston, 1948), pp. 99–128.

[11] A. A. Berle and G. C. Means, *The Modern Corporation and Private Property* (New York: Macmillan, 1947).

of price competition in the classical sense and described the monopoly elements in our markets created by market sharing, price
leadership, and so forth.[12] Gardiner C. Means inaugurated an ex-
tensive literature concerned with measuring the extent of concentration of economic power in the economy of the United States. He
also developed the concept of administered prices, that is, of prices
set by oligopolistic firms with market power which are relatively
insensitive to changes in supply and demand.[13] The insensitivity
of administered prices to market conditions made the idea of a
free market which leads to an optimum allocation of resources
highly questionable. These institutional studies culminated in
the monumental investigation of the concentration of economic
power by a committee of the U.S. Senate in the early 1940's.[14]
Although the value of its findings is somewhat dubious because
of the lack of sufficient theoretical penetration, the statistics and
facts gathered by the TNEC confirmed the oligopolistic character
and the predominance of market power in important sections of
the economy.

These findings were reflected in economic thought, in which
a continuing struggle took place between the laissez-faire philosophy, where moral questions are supposed to be solved by the
market, and the effort to arrive at a normative code for business
behavior and economic action. The magnum opus of Berle and
Means stresses mostly the disintegration of the traditional laissez-
faire philosophy. They try to show that the traditional "logic" of
property and of profits is inadequate to deal with the behavior of
large corporations where management has extricated itself from
control by owner-stockholders. In contrast to the literature on
imperfect and monopolistic competition, they did not confine
themselves to the external effects of market power but, so to speak,
looked inside the corporation. They found the cause of changes in
the free market system in the internal structure of the corporation,

[12] A. R. Burns, *The Decline of Competition* (New York: McGraw-Hill Book Co., 1936).
[13] Gardiner C. Means, *The Corporate Revolution in America* (New York: Collier Books, 1964); *Pricing Power and the Public Interest* (New York: Harper & Brothers, 1962).
[14] Temporary National Economic Committee (TNEC) created pursuant to Public Res. 113, 75th Congress.

especially in the shift of power from owner-stockholders to management. Traditional theory had treated "firms" as indivisible units, as the atom of the economic universe. Berle and Means "split the atom" and discovered that there can be a conflict of interest between management and owner-stockholders. With this step they opened the door for the inclusion of organization theory into economics, a road that was, however, little used by conventional wisdom. Their argument runs essentially like this.[15]

Before the advent of the modern large corporation, entrepreneurial functions were carried out by the same persons, the owner-managers who invested, bore the risks of investment and made all the major and minor decisions about how to manage and administer the business of the firm. This was and is always the case in single proprietorships and in most partnerships. It was also true in smaller corporations and those owned by a few stockholders who also ran the business. With the growing size of corporations, and the growing number of stockholders, necessitated by the increasing capital requirements of a complex technology and business organization, a process of separation of ownership and control set in. The stockholders lost to management the powers of control and decision-making. Berle and Means discuss the numerous legal and organizational steps which brought about this separation of ownership and management control: dispersion of stock ownership, increasing size of corporations, general incorporation laws, vote of stockholders by proxy, restriction of stockholders' rights to remove directors, issuance of nonvoting and nonpar stock, the diminution of the right of stockholders to invest additional moneys in the corporation (preemption rights), and so forth. Berle and Means describe the result of these developments: "the shareholder . . . has surrendered a set of definite rights for a set of indefinite expectations . . . [he] is left . . . with little more than the loose expectation that a group of men (management) under nominal duty to run the enterprise for his benefit . . . will actually observe this obligation. . . . As a result . . . the individual interest of the shareholder is definitely made subservient to the will of a controlling group of managers . . . the interests of the individual

---

[15] Berle and Means, *loc. cit.*, Book IV.

(stockholder) may be sacrificed to the economic exigencies of the enterprise as a whole, the interpretation of the board of directors [or of the president of the corporation] as to what constitutes an economic exigency being practically final." [16]

This created a definitely "undemocratic" situation and reflects a general trend of modern Western society. The separation of ownership and management is a part of the growing separation and distance between the rulers and the ruled, between the lawmakers and the administrators and those who are subject to laws and administrative action. This is not a special problem of the corporate sector of the economy; it is a phenomenon connected with mass society, mass organizations, with bureaucratization, and with the complexity of "advanced" technology. All these factors seem to have generated doubts about the meaning of "representation." How can the representatives, be they elected or appointed public officials, leaders of trade unions or corporate directors and managers, be made more responsible or more responsive to the needs, interests, aspirations, to the "will" of those they represent? But this is instrumental, value-empty reasoning. It does not ask whether the correct representation of the will of the representees by the representatives will accomplish something that is "good." This is left to an invisible hand which is supposed to be at work in politics, in society as a whole as well as in the economy; an invisible hand which somehow miraculously will bring about the good by the integration of individual and specific group interests. It is assumed that representation—political, social and economic—in a democracy requires merely that the representatives should faithfully represent the "will" of the represented, regardless of its content, especially also regardless of its relation to the good. It is an application of Rousseau's concept of the general will.

In *The New Science of Politics*, Erich Voegelin has enlarged the concept of representation beyond its modern democratic content and context. A representative is a person or a group whose acts are experienced by the representees (the members of society) "as the declaration of a rule with obligatory force for themselves." Voegelin makes a clear distinction between an agent and a repre-

---

[16] Berle and Means, *loc. cit.*, pp. 277–78.

sentative: the first is "empowered by his principal to transact a specific business under instructions, while by a representative shall be understood a person who has power to act for a society by virtue of his position in the structure of the community without specific instructions for a specified business." The concept of a representative is not confined to the modern Western democratic forms of representation through elections but includes kings and other rulers or ruling bodies. In the light of a subjective, value-empty concept of the political, social, economic order, such representation appears to be "nondemocratic," that is, nonrepresentative. However, even the acts of an "absolute" ruler, not limited by any legal restrictions or checks and balances, can be quite "representative" for the society he rules and represents if his acts are in conformity with the objective value-system, the social "priorities" of this society; and even a constitutional restricted ruling group, whose legal position comes close to that of an agent, can make decisions which violate the ethical code of those they represent. We have to emancipate ourselves from thinking purely in terms of our own institutions and ideology; the acts of an absolute ruler *could* be more representative and "democratic" than the acts of "democratically elected" representatives, if by "representative" and "democratic" we mean conforming to the values and the ethics of society. Admittedly, we are on dangerous grounds here. The entire democratic tradition is based on the idea of legal and organizational checks and balances of "absolute" rulers; and the introduction of constitutional and other legal restrictions was an important step in the political development in the West. However, under the impact of value-empty subjectivistic reasoning, we have overlooked the fact that the *inner* normative restrictions of rulers and the ruled, based on ethics and morality, are a necessary complement to external restrictions. Only the *combination* of an *internalized value system* and *external checks* can assure that the rulers act in a really representative and democratic way. The "freedom" of democracy was possible only because the Protestant-Puritan ethos was combined with the secular values of honesty, reliability and gentlemanly behavior. The loosening of outer restrictions was made possible by the intensification of inner moral, normative restrictions, or: outer repression could be relaxed because it was partly replaced by inner "repression," a repression which meant the internalization of a moral code. However, today we have, in the West, democratically elected rulers who are mostly motivated by the desire to remain in power and whose actions are not informed by any firm values and convictions about what is right and what is wrong. They try mainly to balance the conflicting interests of many groups so that they will be reelected and can remain in power. Hence, the frequency of corruption, the talking out of both sides of the mouth, the moral inconsistencies and the so-called "credibility gap." The transition from absolutism to democracy in the West during the last two hundred years represents progress, but it has not ensured adequate representation for the people. This is not a plea for a return to benevolent absolutism or dictatorial rule but merely a plea for a less time- and culture-bound approach to the idea of representation and to the idea of political morality.

All this can be applied to the modern Western corporate economy. In the light of the traditional laissez-faire philosophy, the managers are agents for the stockholders; through the separation of management and ownership, they have become "representatives," but representatives without any mechanism through which they can be controlled and made responsible to the stockholders, a point emphasized by Berle and Means. They also point to but do not stress sufficiently the lack of a common ethical guideline by which the managers could be bound, thereby making their actions more "representative." The question raised by Berle and Means—and pursued by the entire literature they have generated—is: Who is representing whom? Should the managers be responsive only to the "will" and interests of the stockholders? Or to their own managerial interests? Or to the interests of all the groups involved in the corporation, such as the labor force, the suppliers, the consumers? [17] Or should they pursue the "interests of the community," the common good? These are exactly the same problems that arose

---

[17] This is the point taken by Carl Kaysen in "The Social Significance of the Modern Corporation," *American Economic Review*, vol. XLVII, no. 2 (May, 1957).

in the political realm: with increasing numbers of participants and an increasingly complex technical, organizational system, the simple direct nexus of represented and representatives has been lost. In predemocratic days, this nexus was established by a common institutionalized belief system; in early democratic days, by the direct democracy of the town meeting; and, later, by a simple electoral system with the voters (like the early stockholders) in direct control. In the twentieth century the directness and simplicity of this nexus was disturbed. Legal and organizational ties between representatives and representees became weaker, and with the evaporation of a common value- and belief system, inner ties vanished. Thus, the search is on not only for new organizational devices but also for a new value system to restore the nexus between the represented and the representatives.

In respect to the relations between stockholders and management, three kinds of answers were given: (1) return control to the owner-stockholders, (2) subject the managers to public control by the community, (3) assume that in practice managers have to balance out the "interests" of all groups involved in the affairs of the corporation, including those of society as a whole. Solution (1) conforms to the laissez-faire philosophy. Solution (2) conforms to the idea that there "is" something like the common good. Solution (3) oscillates between a theory of subjective, value-empty conflict of interests and the idea of a common good.

Those who want to restore control to the stockholders argue that this is necessary to make the free market and enterprise system work. According to Berle and Means the traditional system of private property and of profits (the free market and price system) is justified on functional and moral grounds. The private property holder has to reap the benefits of his ownership; this gives him the incentive to invest, to take risks and to make the decisions which will lead to profits. In such a system " . . . where true private enterprise existed, personal profit was an effective and *socially beneficent* motivating force." [18] The functional *and moral* aspects of the traditional ideology are fully accepted. This is not the

---

[18] Berle and Means, *loc. cit.,* Book IV, p. 350.

formalistic, value-empty concept of laissez-faire. Berle and Means hark back to the *moral* tradition of classical economics.

However, they deny the applicability of this philosophy to the modern corporation with its separation of ownership from management; the mechanism of property rights and rewards does not work anymore for the public benefit when owners and managers are different groups. If the rewards (profits) accrue to the noncontrolling owners only, the decision-making managers will not be motivated to exert themselves to the utmost. The modern corporation where ownership and decision-making are in separate hands is like the whipping boy of the medieval princes: the prince sins and the whipping boy is punished; the managers make the wrong decisions and the stockholders suffer the losses; also the managers are not those who receive the profits, when they have made the right decisions. Therefore, these managers are insufficiently motivated to be as ardent in the pursuit of profits and the avoidance of losses as the owners. Also, since competition among giants is ineffective and there is considerable market power, there is no mechanism or procedure which restrains the powers of management in the market.

This is another cause for the growing indeterminateness of markets with large corporations (see above pp. 118 ff.). Since the owners are no longer the ones who make the decisions, how can the decision makers be made to aim at nothing but profit maximization? The striving for profit maximization is the precondition for a determinate equilibrium theory. The separation of management and ownership destroys this possibility.

Berle and Means reject both control by the property owners and leaving uncurbed powers in the hands of the controlling managers. They assert that this situation has "placed the community in a position to demand that the modern corporation serve not alone the owners or the managers but all society"—in other words, the common good. This is a clear-cut return to political economy and to the search for normative goals and ideals in economics.

E. S. Mason has demonstrated the need for a system that could explain and justify the economy with corporate power. ". . . it seems to be a fact that the institutional stability and opportunity for growth of an economic system are heavily dependent on the existence of a philosophy or ideology justifying the system in a manner generally acceptable to the leaders of thought in a community. Classical economics in the form of a 'philosophy of natural liberty' performed that function admirably for the nineteenth century capitalism." [19] Mason points out that classical economics provided not only an explanation but also a defense of the free enterprise system by maintaining that it works in the public interest. He concludes ". . . that the growth of nineteenth century capitalism depended largely on the general acceptance of a reasoned justification of the system on moral as well as on political and economic grounds." The free enterprise system was considered to be morally justified because it offered individuals maximum opportunities to increase their incomes, because it supposedly led to distributive justice by rewarding the owners of all factors of production according to the value of their productive contribution, and because it allocated resources in the "best" way.

Nowhere has the necessity of a central belief system with a *moral* content been made so clear. Here, the laissez-faire philosophy is defended—although Mason, in the end, asks for a new philosophy more adequate for the facts of corporate power and the separation of management and ownership—not because it is "true" and corresponds to the "facts" of economic life but because of its ideological adequacy. According to Mason—and he is quite right on that point—the managerial literature does not provide a viable ideology and philosophy which would legitimize the overwhelming powers of the management of large corporations. Arguments used to justify a laissez-faire system cannot be applied to the corporate economy. The independent managers of large corporations are not compelled to make the most efficient use of resources; they are not forced to *maximize* profits; they have alternative choices (within certain limits). Upward mobility, necessary in a competitive economy, is hampered by corporate bureaucracy, by the difficulty of entering industries which require a large initial

---

[19] E. S. Mason, "The Apologetics of Managerialism," *Journal of Business of the University of Chicago*, vol. XXX, no. 1 (January, 1958).

investment, and by the monopolistic policies of the large existing corporations aimed at keeping out competition. The corporate economy certainly does not guarantee a just distribution of income. Even if every person received an income that corresponded to his productive contribution (technically the value of his marginal product), this would not necessarily be a just income because of social and other obstacles to occupational mobility: the ditchdigger cannot easily become a surgeon and the inability of the ghetto dweller to move out and upward is well known. Private and public economic functions are no longer clearly separated; the functions of government and industry are thoroughly interdependent in armaments, space exploration, land, air and water transportation, and related fields. Last but not least consumer-sovereignty has been destroyed, or at least restricted by advertising and the stimulation of demand by producers.

All this has been widely discussed in the managerial literature. What is important here is less the truth-value of these various contentions than the shift of debate from the factual to the ideological level. For Mason it is the ideological efficiency of the traditional competitive model that counts; and he criticizes the managerial philosophy for its *ideological* inefficiency. Ideological efficiency means the ability of a system of thought not only to explain but to justify and to legitimize reality. Thus, the truth-value of a system of economic thought ceases to be the criterion of its validity and is replaced by its power to justify. This process reflects what we have said about alienation: the repression of the normative, of the ethical and of morality is now negated, and a search for a new economic morality is instituted.

Mason's arguments still show a mixture of the "factual," "scientific" with the normative approach. He measures managerial economics by the alleged standards of the "philosophy of natural liberty." He maintains that the laissez-faire philosophy has a "reasoned answer" to questions about the beneficiality of the system and the managerial philosophy has not. This, however, is a *petitio principii;* but it is illuminating for the implicit philosophical background of the entire debate between economic libertarian and orthodox economists on the one hand, and managerialists on the other. The free competitive market is assumed to perform certain functions in a beneficial way: optimum allocation of resources and just and fair incomes; economic libertarians stress that there are no socioeconomic mechanisms that would force corporate managers to achieve similar goals. But the *real* situation is that the laissez-faire philosophy interprets the economy in such a way that it *appears* to lead to beneficial results; and what the managerialists are doing is to show that the king has no clothes, that with market power beneficial results are not guaranteed, although it is very doubtful that they were ever guaranteed by a competitive free market economy. These beneficial effects were mostly ideological fictions of the free enterprise philosophy. The managerial theory dispensed with those fictions; but it developed few concepts of its own which could be used to legitimize and justify the corporate state, hence its ideological inadequacy as stressed by Mason.

GOALS OF CORPORATE MANAGEMENT
AND THE REINTRODUCTION OF MORALITY

With the recognition of managerial market power the behavior of corporate managers became the object of study. In the ensuing discussion the opposition between instrumental, value-empty and normative reasoning occurs once again. Instrumental reasoning tries to understand the behavior of managers using instruments of the "scientific" method. In contrast, the new point of view transcends the boundaries of economics. Mason believes that "an effective new ideology" will have to be devised not by economists who "are still too mesmerized with . . . the concept of the market but by psychologists, sociologists and, possibly, political scientists." [20] This is a change of stance, a wider viewpoint but not a new approach. What Mason (and many others) are searching for is a new value system which would not only explain but legitimize and justify the corporate economy. He assumes that a broader frame of reference, including not only economic but psychological, social and political factors, would explain managerial be-

[20] *Ibid.*, p. 11.

havior by a new theory; but such a theory still explains merely by causes and not by ends. It is assumed that the competitive market system allows only economic factors such as prices, costs, profits and so forth to operate, whereas the corporate economy opens the door to many more extraeconomic factors. If they are taken into account, the result will still be determinate. The new managerial theory is as deterministic as the laissez-faire philosophy; it only takes into account more variables, some of them noneconomic ones.

One formulation of the new managerial theory is an enlargement of the agency theory of management. Under the traditional logic of property and profits, the managers were considered as the agents of the owners. The new theory postulates that the managers of large corporations have a "diffuse and undefined responsibility to workers, suppliers, customers, and the general public." [21]

In the words of Carl Kaysen:

> Management sees itself as responsible to stockholders, employees, customers, the general public, and perhaps most important, the firm itself as an institution. . . . Its responsibilities to the general public are widespread: leadership in local charitable enterprises, concern with factory architecture and landscaping, provision of support for higher education, and even research in pure science, to name a few. To the firm itself, as an institution, the management owes the primary responsibility of insuring the maintenance and, if possible, the expansion of its long-run position; in other words, sustained and rapid growth.[22]

This approach is a mixture of "scientific" and normative reasoning. Sometimes it is formulated as a "balance of social pressures" theory: corporate management is subject to pressures from all of these groups and interests and has to establish some balance of these interests. Thus, managerial action becomes a sort of a "parallelogram of forces." Its actions would not be informed by any general goals in conformity with certain values or by what is right but would be determined by conflicting group pressures. This approach can also be found in political science and sociology wherein the American political system is seen as a balance of pressure—or veto groups

[21] *Ibid.*, p. 6.
[22] Carl Kaysen, *loc. cit.*, p. 313.

whose interests have to be balanced by the Federal Government.[23] According to this approach both corporate management and government do not have to do what is right but have merely to balance conflicting interests. This is, in part, still a relativistic, value-empty theory informed by technical formal reason like the free market theory. Like this theory it relies on a mechanism: not competition, but the pressure of group interests.

This theory has not only been applied to the internal situation of the corporation and the relations between management and the various groups directly interested in corporate action but also to the entire market situation in Galbraith's theory of countervailing power.[24] Price competition between small firms was supposed to be the factor which restricted the market power of firms in the laissez-faire system; this is competition on the same side of the market, between sellers or between buyers. In markets with large powerful firms "private economic power is held in check by the countervailing power of those who are subject to it." [25] Powerful sellers of processed meat encounter powerful chain stores. Powerful employers of labor generate powerful union organizations. There is a tendency in the corporate sector of the modern economy for original power to generate countervailing power.

This is a mechanical, instrumental, deterministic, value-empty theory which rests on the same philosophical and methodological basis as the value-relativistic free market theory. In both cases the market is regulated by an automatic equilibrating force: competition in one case, countervailing power in the other. The latter is a more realistic model than the competitive one, more appropriate for a society and economy dominated by large powerful groups and organizations to which the "balance of power" scheme is eminently applicable. (It should be pointed out that in his *Affluent Society*, Galbraith chose an entirely different approach; in his theory of the social balance [chap. XVIII] he makes concrete

---

[23] David Riesman, *The Lonely Crowd*, pp. 242 ff.
[24] J. K. Galbraith, *American Capitalism: The Concept of Countervailing Power*, rev. ed. (Boston: Houghton Mifflin, 1956), especially chap. IX.
[25] *Ibid.*, p. 111.

substantial value judgments about economic goals. See below pp. 160 ff.).

These more realistic views of the corporate economy led to doubts about the ubiquity of the profit motive. Actually, the profit motive was not the only driving force at work in the history of Western capitalism. This history can be viewed as a struggle between the free self-regulating market, working like a cybernetic system on the one hand, and "social protectionism" on the other hand. Social protectionism consists of legal and administrative measures which protected the human substance and the environment against the destructive effects of the free market.[26]

In the social legislation regulating child labor, the working day, working conditions, health insurance, workmen's compensation, and so forth, the pursuit of profit was restricted to protect the interests of certain disadvantaged groups. In nineteenth-century England and on the Continent, the beginnings of such social control were the creation of a public, service-minded bureaucracy, supported by remnants of a feudal, noneconomic ethos; in Britain, by the ideal of the gentleman and on the Continent, by the paternalistic tradition of the aristocracy and of enlightened absolutism. In other words, capitalist society rested, from its very beginnings, on two normative principles which were in dialectical juxtaposition: the acquisitive attitude in the free market on the one hand, and social protectionism for the sake of the common good on the other hand. In the fight against poverty and exploitation, in compassion for the "underdog," there was, and is, an element of objective reason, derived from a concept of the good which survived, in spite of the acquisitive ethos and, later, in spite of the ethical neutrality and value-emptiness of the free market philosophy. The politicians and administrators who introduced factory legislation, workmen's compensation, municipalization of utilities and many other laws of social protection did so not under political pressure but informed by concepts of the common good. The gentlemen of the English bureaucracy felt a responsibility for the lower classes for moral reasons.

---

[26] K. Polanyi, *The Great Transformation* (New York: Farrar & Rinehart 1944, Beacon Paperback, 1957).

These normative elements were revived in the managerial literature. The managerial philosophy shows a combination of three points of view: (1) a clearly normative approach, with a call for a new moral code; (2) a balance-of-interest approach; and (3) the discovery of normative goals in the motives of the managers. These trends are manifest in discussions about the declining importance of the profit motive. It is believed that owners are interested in profits, in an increase in their equity, and in an increase in the price of their stocks, whereas managers are more interested in security, stability and smoothness of operation. Owners would resist an increase in labor costs caused by union demands to the utmost. Managers may be more inclined to be conciliatory; after all, they have to work with the union day by day. The fact that in the 1930's the industrial unionism of the CIO was finally accepted by U.S. Steel, managed by corporate bureaucrats, after it was fought tooth and nail by smaller, owner-operated steel firms, may support this point.

Whether managers are less interested in profits than owners seems to have little connection with the fight among economists over the concept of profit *maximization*. This concept is based entirely on the traditional model of the firm's behavior which assumes that by producing an output which guarantees the maximum profits under the given cost and demand conditions the firm will reach an equilibrium. The real situation seems to be that firms aim at profits; sometimes, and for various reasons, at *higher* profits but not necessarily at *maximum* profits. Because of the uncertainty of the future and the lack of knowledge of what would have happened if an alternative policy had been chosen, a firm can never know for sure whether it has *maximized* profits.

However, the discussion in managerial economics centers primarily around the question whether corporate managers *maximize* profits (as the firm in free competitive markets is supposed to do) or whether they pursue other goals. What is at stake here is really much more than a discussion about a correct interpretation of managerial behavior. It is probably true that economic action, even under a relatively free competitive market system, was always motivated by a great variety of motives in addition to the acquisitive attitude: custom, habit, altruism, friendship, morality probably always restricted the extreme pursuit of gain. The competitive struggle used to resemble a boxing match under Marquess of Queensberry rules rather than an all-out fight with no holds barred. The repression of the normative, however, has obscured this fact; and the revival of normative reasoning has made nonacquisitive motives and goals visible again. Berle and Means stress the social responsibility of management. Carl Kaysen lists such corporate goals as being a high-wage employer, maintaining good community relations, supporting liberal arts education, and describes Standard Oil of New Jersey, American Telephone and Telegraph, DuPont, General Electric, General Motors as "soulful corporations." [27] These statements are more than a factual description, for as facts they are doubtful; as an indication of a trend they are symptomatic and significant. These and similar passages indicate a change in the value system: a weakening, a dilution, a restriction of the acquisitive attitude and a revival of social conscience.

All this did not solve the problem of legitimizing and justifying the system of corporate and managerial power on moral grounds and from the viewpoint of the common good. However, A. A. Berle has raised this moral problem in the most unequivocal fashion.[28] He clearly confronts the question of the legitimacy of power. Referring to the situation in the early Middle Ages when "lords spiritual" had moral power over the "lords temporal," he invokes "conceptions of right, of morality and justice" from which even the absolute kings were not exempted and to which the "temporal" managers of corporation should also be subject.[29] In England, in the Middle Ages, relief against inequities was granted by the king in Chancery based on equity against the iniquities of common law. Such decisions were based on the "conscience of the king" and on the conviction that "somewhere, somehow, there is

---

[27] Kaysen, *loc. cit.*, p. 314.

[28] A. A. Berle, Jr., *Economic Power and the Free Society* (Santa Barbara, Calif.: Center for the Study of Democratic Institutions, 1957); *The 20th Century Capitalist Revolution* (New York: Harcourt, Brace & World, 1954); *The American Economic Republic* (New York: Harcourt, Brace & World, 1963); *Power Without Property* (New York: Harcourt, Brace, 1959).

[29] Berle, *The 20th Century Capitalist Revolution*, p. 63; and *Economic Power and the Free Society*, pp. 16 ff.

a higher law which imposes itself in time on . . . powers . . . of
this . . . earth" [30]

This is an open appeal to moral principles (in the form of
natural law or the natural right). Berle expects to see the development of a moral conscience or of a normative code of behavior
for management which would eventually emerge as law. He rejects the idea that the new morality could harmonize corporation
and society, corporate activities and prevailing ethical ideas.
Ethics is supposed to check power, not to harmonize with it. Berle's
cry for a corporate conscience is a cry for a moral code, for normative guidelines, for a reorientation of economic reasoning in a
normative direction. His conclusion is that "it seems, the corporations have a conscience, or else should accept direction from the
conscience of the government. This conscience must be built into
institutions so that it can be invoked as a right by the individuals
and interests, subject to the corporate power." He clearly considers corporate powers in trust, not for shareholders but for the
entire community, that is, for the common good.[31]

We are presenting these ideas not merely for their immanent
validity (although we agree with Berle) but because they are a
symptom of the new normative approach in economics. Berle was
a distinguished public servant, a lawyer and political scientist and
not an economist. Nevertheless his approach is reflected in the
entire managerial literature and is also in line with some of
Galbraith's ideas. One can have doubts about the possibility of
generating a corporate conscience based on a moral code supported
by laws; there can be little doubt about the desirability of such a
development. However, one must recognize that instrumental,
value-empty reasoning in economics is one of the greatest obstacles
in the path of such a development. As long as economists view the
economy as a cybernetic system in which suprapersonal forces will
automatically lead to beneficial results—a point of view taken over
from the laissez-faire philosophy in its value-relativistic form—any
restriction of corporate power will lack a philosophical basis. This
is the case whether the automatic self-regulating system is viewed

---

[30] Berle, *The 20th Century Capitalist Revolution*, p. 69.
[31] *Ibid.*, pp. 113–14, 169.

as a competitive market system, or as a system of balance involving opposed interests or powers. Any restriction of power by tradition, customs, mores, implicit or explicit rules and laws must rest on deeply rooted convictions about right and wrong. Without such convictions the effort to improve public services, control armaments, population, pollution, and urbanization, and so forth lacks any philosophical and ideological basis. The striving for economic justice will require that intellectuals concern themselves not only with the common good but with the good itself, with what is right and what is wrong. Instrumental, formalized, value-empty reasoning has corrupted intellectuals, academicians, scientists and made it difficult for them to use reason in the search for a new morality. This was (and to a large extent still is) especially true of economists.[32]

THE NEW INDUSTRIAL STATE

The most recent changes in the corporate sector and in the structure of management have been described and analyzed brilliantly in J. K. Galbraith, *The New Industrial State*.[33] He continues and elaborates on ideas that have been discussed in the managerial literature since the 1930's: (1) He describes the demise of the competitive free market because of all-inclusive corporate planning; (2) He discovers a new subgroup within the managerial elite which he calls the techno-structure; (3) Above all—and this is a new line of thought—he attributes the social goals of untrammeled economic growth and technological change to the influence of the corporate techno-structure.

Galbraith restricts his analysis to those parts of the economy in which the modern large corporation is the most conspicuous manifestation: "nearly all communications, nearly all production and distribution of electric power, much transportation, most manufacturing and mining, a substantial share of retail trade, and a

---

[32] Heilbroner has repeatedly advocated a reorientation of economics in the direction of goal-oriented political economics; see especially "On the Possibility of a Political Economics," *Journal of Economic Issues*, vol. IV, no. 4 (December, 1970); this is an appeal to include normative elements in economics.

[33] Boston: Houghton Mifflin, 1967.

considerable amount of entertainment." Smaller scale firms are still found in "agriculture, truck mines, professions, handicrafts, some retail trade" and in many services.[34] The industrial system dominated by large corporations is the carrier of modern technological change. Technology requires large capital investment and complex organizational structures. This, in turn, necessitates ubiquitous planning at every step: from the planning of savings, investment, research and development, the supply of factors, to final sales (through advertising). Large-scale investment is a long-run process that could be endangered by the vagaries of the market. Technology, planning and coordination of all the subdivisions of skills, knowledge, machines and men require the activities of the techno-structure comprising "all who bring specialized knowledge, talent or experience to group decision making . . . the guiding intelligence—the brain—of the enterprise." [35]

This new "ruling group" exercising power in the present-day large corporation represents a new stage in the development of capitalist decision-making groups: first the owner-entrepreneur, then corporate management with control divorced from ownership and finally, a subgroup within management consisting of all kinds of experts in science, technology, psychology, marketing, personnel, organization, administration and communication. This techno-structure within the corporation is socially in contact with education and research scientists, with civil servants, journalists, writers, artists outside.[36] Together they form an educational and scientific estate whose prestige derives from the productive agent they supply, namely knowledge, information, expertise, manipulative and organizational skills. This group holds power because they are the basic "scarce factor" in the new industrial state (chaps. X to XV). They are doing the necessary planning which they control by their expertise.

Emphasis on corporate planning is another way to talk about the replacement of the invisible hand of the market by the visible hand of corporate management; but the power of management

---

[34] *The New Industrial State*, p. 9.
[35] *Ibid.*, p. 71.
[36] *Ibid.*, p. 782.

and the function of planning have now shifted to a managerial subgroup, to the techno-structure. This shift in power, control and decision making has further undermined the idea that "compulsive profit maximization" [37] is the goal of all corporations. The techno-structure is even less interested in profit maximization than are the managers. The members of the techno-structure are salaried employees, with little or no stock ownership and profit-related bonuses. They get even less of the profits they allegedly maximize than top management. If there ever was a danger that corporate power would be abused for personal enrichment by an independent irresponsible management, this danger "disappeared as power passed into the techno-structure." [38]

Although Galbraith agrees with the idea that the market power of large corporations permits them to pursue goals other than profit maximization and although he does not entirely reject the idea that sometimes social purpose and the common good inform corporate policies, his emphasis is on the use of power by the techno-structure. "Exercise of power . . . is also power to pursue other goals . . . to serve the deeper interests or goals of the techno-structure . . ." [39]

Thus, we have to search for these deeper interests of the techno-structure, which leads Galbraith into the dense underbrush of motivation theory to examine the motivations of members of an organization. However, what he calls motivations are rather mechanisms by which the goals of individuals are adjusted to the goals of the corporation, or by which the two sets of goals are brought closer together. They are socializing mechanisms rather than motivations. Galbraith distinguishes compulsion, pecuniary rewards, identification of individuals with organizational goals, and adaptation of organizational to individual goals.[40] Compulsion has become less important in democratic, urbanized societies. Affluence has reduced the importance of the pecuniary reward. "The paradox of pecuniary motivation is that . . . the higher the

---

[37] *Ibid.*, p. 112.
[38] *Ibid.*, p. 120.
[39] *Ibid.*, pp. 126–27.
[40] *Ibid.*, pp. 130 ff.

amount, the less the importance in relation to other motivations." [41]
Thus, within the techno-structure, identification and adaptation as
socializing mechanisms are of increasing importance. Identification
is a typically other-directed technique of socialization within an
organization. It is the "collectivist" technique par excellence. In
contrast to isolated individualistic pursuit of gain, members of an
organization are supposed to receive their inner strength through
identification with the organization. If Galbraith is right, and there
is little doubt that he is, the other-directed and collectivistic character of the large "mature" corporation is obvious. However,
identification with a collectivity can also be a source of alienation
if the needs and goals of the individual cannot be fully identified
with the goals of the organization. If individual and social goals
are in harmony and identical with the goals of the large corporations, individual identification with these goals is facilitated.
Galbraith believes that such a threefold identification of individual,
corporate and social goals may be taking place in the new industrial state and that the goals of society may have become identical
with the goals of the mature corporation, under the impact of
persuasion by the techno-structure. The harmony of corporate
and social goals is being established by corporate planning, and the
deliberate creation of a consensus on goals.

Galbraith considers as the goals of the large corporation and its
techno-structure: survival and autonomy. Their achievement requires profits sufficient to pacify the stockholders and to supply
savings for reinvestment, with minimum interference by governments. The large corporation also aims at a large growth rate
measured in sales as a protection against loss of market power. The
techno-structure is greatly interested in the use of technical virtuosity for the purposes of innovation and growth.[42] Secondary goals
of a social nature such as community building, improved education, and so forth, and the creation of a favorable image of the
corporation, support these primary goals of autonomy, growth
and technical innovation, and serve to persuade society of the inherent "goodness" of the large corporation.

[41] *Ibid.*, p. 137.
[42] *Ibid.*, chap. XV.

The goals of economic growth and technical innovation have, under the impact of corporate ideology, become social goals as well. The economic growth imperative and the imperative of technological change are the most important dynamic factors in present Western and especially in American society. This is the new morality that has replaced the value-relativism of welfare economics. These imperatives seem to have a substantial, concrete objective content. The growth imperative implies that the volume and variety of goods and services, regardless of what they consist of, should continuously rise from year to year; the technological imperative means that everything that *can* be *should* be invented and produced. Economic growth and technical progress become ends in themselves—ends of the techno-structure, of the corporations and of society as a whole. This seems to be the new harmony and the new consensus which has replaced the harmony of natural interests of the free market. It seems that the value-relativism and the value-emptiness of neoclassical and welfare economics were overcome in managerial economic philosophy by substantial "values" in the form of economic growth and the technological imperative. Lately, however, as a reaction to the wide acceptance of this ideal of economic growth, a trend has developed which criticizes such an ideal from the point of view of the common good and basic human needs.

6

GNP-Fetishism:
A Critique of Economic Growth

Economic growth as an ideal puts into focus all the deficiencies of economic thought we have discussed. It represents an attempt to combine the value-empty, ethically neutral approach of normative relativism with a concrete, quantitatively measurable yardstick for economic beneficiality. It tries to establish a measure for what is economically good for individuals and for society as a whole. It tries to interpret economic growth as an increase in human need satisfaction. All these justifications are inappropriate to the present situation in Western capitalist societies.

However, there is little disagreement among economists, businessmen and politicians about the desirability of aggregate growth of the economy, defined as an ever-increasing national income or product. In simple language: the goal of the economy is assumed to be a continuous increase in the volume and variety of goods and services per head of the population (without regard to the distribution of these goods and services). In line with the value-emptiness of the free market philosophy, what is produced is much less important than the index of aggregate economic growth, the Gross

National Product (GNP) which is a statistically sophisticated measurement of the total dollar-value of all goods and services produced in a given year.

There are differences among economists about the techniques of national income accounting and serious differences about the means of accomplishing economic growth, but the desirability of overall growth has, until recently, hardly been questioned. A GNP growing, if possible, at an increasing rate has become a dogma of economic reasoning and a center of economic worship. This obsessive preoccupation with growth and the rate of growth of the GNP one could call *GNP-fetishism.* GNP figures, conjectural and tentative at best, are watched by businessmen and politicians alike. Their decline, or allegedly insufficient rate of rise, is considered a national calamity. Comparison of the growth rates of Eastern and Western nations has become a part of the Cold War and a matter of international competition.

Preoccupation with economic growth thus defined has been fostered since the 1930's by the growing popularity of Keynesian economics which shifted the emphasis from price movements on particular markets, caused by changes in supply and demand, to economic aggregates such as total production, employment, investment, saving and overall spending. The accumulation and refinement of aggregate statistics by governmental agencies facilitated the observation of overall economic trends. Preoccupation with economic growth was also stimulated in the post-World War II period by a growing concern with the industrialization of underdeveloped countries, and a new discipline of developmental economics emerged.

However, the roots of the growth mania go deeper; it has earlier historical, philosophical and psychological sources. Historically, it originated in early capitalism and in classical economics, especially with the ideas of Adam Smith about what constitutes the wealth of nations. Philosophically, it is connected with ideas about scarcity and need satisfaction which were developed by the neoclassical school and its later followers. Psychologically, it tries to provide a meaning for economic activity.

What Bertrand de Jouvenel called "la civilisation de toujours plus," the civilization of more and more, rests on an attitude already adopted by individuals in early capitalism in the form of the Protestant-Puritan ethic. We have seen that classical economics also implied this attitude. The classics, especially Adam Smith, developed the foundation on which the ideal of an ever-increasing GNP is based. They interpreted a unique historical phenomenon, the acquisitive orientation, as a universal human inclination, thus making it acceptable as a goal of life.

The idea of economic growth was born as an ethical and psychological orientation of individuals; but for reasons of apologetics, the individual ideal of acquisition was projected into the social sphere and became an ideal for society as a whole. Ideas of economic growth on the individual and on the social level are projections of the ethics of acquisition. This has often been lost sight of in discussions about economic growth because it has become an unconsciously accepted value. It is discussed not from the ethical and psychological but from the functional point of view. The pursuit of economic growth has been rationalized by arguments that it is necessary for full employment, for greater equality, for the elimination of poverty; whether it should be a basic value has not been questioned until very recently.

Still, the desirability of economic growth, of more and more, regardless of what it consists of, is widely maintained. That this should be so is somewhat puzzling because economic thought has developed two central ideas: the idea of continuous economic expansion and growth on the one hand, and the idea of *equilibrium*, a balance of opposing forces, on the other. The idea of acquisitive growth was perhaps appropriate in the earlier stages of capitalism where the main problem was to eliminate the scarcity of goods through increased production, saving, reinvestment and capital. However, when the Western economies became capital-rich and acquired a large productive capacity, problems of marketing and selling became more acute. Selling more and more to consumers involves the problem of satiation, which is represented in economic thought by the concept of "declining marginal utility." It assumes that the urgency of a need declines with increasing satisfaction and that it is possible to reach a point of satiation and saturation; people can have enough and even too much of a good thing (negative marginal utility). This idea arose and became the center of economic thought at a time when the problem of selling the products and determining the consumers' wants became important; therefore Marshall, first among the authors of *Principles of Economics*, included in his work a section on "Wants and Their Satisfaction." This is where he applies the concept of equilibrium. His idea of equilibrium as applied to the consumer contains elements borrowed from physics. He thinks of equilibrium as "balancing opposing forces . . ." and compares it "to the mechanical equilibrium of a stone hanging by an elastic string, or a number of balls resting against one another in a basin." [1] The emphasis shifts to biological and psychological factors when Marshall talks about the "boy who picks blackberries for his own eating . . . Equilibrium is reached when at last his eagerness to play and his disinclination for the work of picking counterbalance the desire for eating." [2] Here physiological and psychological forces lead to an equilibrium situation. This analysis is based on the idea of declining marginal utility which implies physiological and psychological satiation.

The equilibrium of the consumer and the worker who stops working when he feels that his needs are provided for, a physiological and psychological equilibrium, is a *temporary* state of saturation. It is modeled according to the pattern of physiological needs and their satisfaction. There is the "pain" of tension which is then relieved by the "pleasure" of need satisfaction. There is, however, a general trend in economics (and in psychology) to interpret *all* needs according to this pattern. The physiological needs are appetites caused by an actual physical need or lack in the body; the drives "aim" at procuring what is lacking and thereby move toward a state of saturation and equilibrium. Such states of equilibrium are temporary; tension arises again and again in the life history of the organism or individual, to be eliminated again and again by need satisfaction leading to equilibrium.

Equilibrium in general, even temporary equilibrium as a goal

---

[1] *Principles of Economics*, 8th edition, p. 323.
[2] *Ibid.*, p. 331.

of individual economic activity, is incompatible with the ideal of economic growth insofar as it implies ever-rising "individual standards of living." If a point of satiation and full satisfaction is reached, further increase in the volume of goods and services at the disposal of an individual is undesirable. Economic activity would then consist of a metabolic cycle of production, consumption, digestion which could be eternally repeated at the same level without any increase, without any economic growth.

Economic growth is a social concept; it implies an increasing national product. However, in order to be socially desirable it must also be beneficial for each individual. If each individual could reach a point where "more means less" (more goods and services yield less utility or satisfaction) economic growth would be desirable neither for individuals nor for a nation. The question arises whether economic growth, increasing standards of living, are desirable for individuals as a long-run lifetime goal. There is a conflict between this goal and the idea of balance, equilibrium and satiation. On the one hand, human life can be interpreted as a Faustian struggle for more and more; on the other hand, as the striving for a point "of repose and continuance," a target income which, once achieved, is experienced as an equilibrated situation in which further economic advance is less important than peace of mind, rest, contemplation, enjoyment and leisure. If that could be true of an individual, it can also be true of a nation; beyond a certain point an increase in the GNP may be undesirable.

ECONOMIC GROWTH AND NEED SATISFACTION

The conflict between the concept of economic growth and the concept of an equilibrium of satisfaction reflects an inner conflict in modern capitalism. As we have seen, its last phase, the corporate state, elevated economic growth together with technological innovation to the dignity of an ideal. At the same time, economics, the self-interpretation of this society, maintained that the economy, including the giant corporations, serve the satisfaction of human needs. If such satisfaction depends on the achievement of an equilibrium, of a balance, of satiation and contentment, the corporate and national striving for more and more would, at some point, become meaningless. Therefore, economists have tried to combine the two incompatible concepts by trying to establish a *need* for unlimited economic growth, and thus give it a meaning and justification. This was done by trying to identify needs in general with "natural" physiological needs and, in turn, to present the idea of continuous economic growth as rooted in nature.

The reason for this approach can be found in the naturalistic, scientistic style of economic thought and in its ideological implications. If something can be explained as "natural," as rooted in biological instincts, drives or needs, it is, in a scientific culture, implicitly justified. Implicitly economists assume that needs are given by nature, originating with the individual, and that production and the economic system serve to satisfy those needs.

This situation, however, is by no means universal; it is abstracted from primitive economics where mere subsistence is the goal of economic action. It existed in all economies where agriculture is the main economic activity and it exists in some of the most underdeveloped countries today. In such situations the goal of economic activity is survival. Human needs here are, indeed, "given" by biological necessity. Here, man is subject to the dire necessity of working and economizing. Only these activities ensure his survival. Here, economic activity is part of the metabolic cycle of life; production, consumption, digestion, fertilization and renewed production follow each other in a never-ending cycle.[3] They are subject to the laws of nature. As far as economic activity was unavoidable through the pressure of necessity, it did not require any formulation of goals for its justification or meaning. It is in the nature of an automatic movement, such as the beating of the heart. Only insofar as economic activity produces a surplus over and above the bare necessities for survival does it enter the realm of freedom and require meaningful justification. This meaning was, in preindustrial society, created by religious, social and political institutions in which the economic activity was embedded. The surplus was used for the purposes of groups which were the

---

[3] H. Arendt, *The Human Condition*, Part III.

carriers of the world outlook and meaning of their societies. The surplus over and above the means of subsistence and the economic activity producing it were considered as means to noneconomic ends and received their meaning from religious, social and political institutions. This may very well be the only meaningful evaluation of economic activity; as far as it is not subject to necessity, it can only receive a meaning from something that is beyond the economic dimension. Otherwise, economic activity becomes meaningless.

In order to avoid this result and in the absence of a superordinated system of noneconomic values in Western society, economic thought tried to reduce all economic activity to the level of physiological need satisfaction. If everything we are producing, selling and consuming today in the advanced complex Western economies could be interpreted as satiating a quasi-physiological drive or need, our economic activity would need no further justification.

The physiological interpretation of need satisfaction presupposes a state of tension which is relieved by satisfaction. Without the emergence of tension, no satisfaction can be received from physiological need satisfaction. Without hunger the intake of food is not pleasurable. This statement is so trite that one hesitates to make it. However, this obvious truth is overlooked when it comes to an evaluation of economic acquisition and growth. The principle of declining marginal utility can be applied not only to specific kinds of needs and their satisfaction but also to the entire field of acquisition of goods and services which are produced by our economy.[4]

The affluent industrial economy has immensely enlarged the field of "need satisfaction" and raised so-called standards of living to a peak that was never reached before. We have come such a long way that many social scientists and philosophers talk about an imminent state of affairs in which men will be freed of economic necessity altogether by automation and cybernation of production. They predict that, in the foreseeable future, man in the advanced

---

[4] See Galbraith, *The Affluent Society,* chap. X.

industrial economy may be able to make the "leap from the realm of necessity into the realm of freedom." However that may be, even at the present time, the advanced Western economies have reached a level of production which has reduced immensely the importance of acquiring more and more additional goods and services of the traditional variety. This is not a situation of which people are conscious. The ideology of "more and more" is still so strong that people are precluded from becoming aware of the fact that they are forced into more work and more acquisition by the socioeconomic system rather than by their free inclination. Intensive advertising and the all-prevasive fact of artificial obsolescence are clear and present symptoms of this situation. Artificial obsolescence through planned change is the social correlate to the emergence of tension in the physiological field. *Nolens volens,* people get hungry. Planned obsolescence replaces physiological tension in those fields where no natural automatic tension arises. What firms and advertisers are doing is to create hunger where nature has not provided for such an incidence. Through frequently changing styles of cars and clothes, and by exploiting the desire for conformity, they "force" people to develop a "need" for change much like the need for food that arises automatically for physiological reasons. The same purpose is accomplished by the continuous development of new products and new kinds of need satisfaction. Once the new product and the new kind of "need" is marketed, the pressure of conformity actually creates a "need." This is the way in which business practice and economic thought try to combine a restrictive natural physiological interpretation of needs with the idea of economic growth. The physiological pattern of recurrent tension is artificially reproduced, thereby representing economic growth as the result of "natural" physiological forces. That purely physical and sensual pleasure requires ever more excitation and titillation, tension and pain, was known not only to the Hindus and Buddhists but also to the Greek philosophers of the Periclean and Hellenistic periods. It was, of course, known to Christian thought from the Fathers of the Church to the Middle Ages. All these cultures saw virtue in balance and moderation, or even in restraint and negation of desires. Modern civilization, however, has elevated the continuous creation of tension for the sake of pleasurable "satisfaction" to the dignity of an ultimate goal. Economic growth as an individual and social ideal seems justified if this constant creation of new "needs" can be viewed as a continuation of a natural process. However, what is overlooked is that in nature a point of satiation is reached, whereas, in the affluent economy, this is prevented by the continuous creation of new "needs."

CONSUMERS' NEEDS AND CONSUMERS'
SOVEREIGNTY

The physiological pattern for economic activity has also been used as an argument in favor of the free market. Physiological needs originate with the individual. If all needs were of the same nature as the physiological ones, one could argue that all consumer demands originate with him. If one assumes that a free competitive market leads to the maximum possible satisfaction of such needs originating with the individual, the free market is justified because it allegedly assures what economists like to call *consumers' sovereignty*. If such sovereignty is accepted as a goal, economic systems will have to be evaluated according to the degree to which they satisfy the original individual needs of consumers. The idea that consumers' needs and wants originating with them should be satisfied and that "the consumer should be king" is almost universally accepted in traditional economic theory. In the continuously raging discussion about the relative merits of a free competitive market versus an economy planned by government agencies and/or large corporations, all parties to the dispute assume that an economic system is beneficial if consumers are sovereign so that they determine what is being produced and thus get their demands satisfied. Laissez-faire economists assume that a free market guarantees this sovereignty. Their antagonists try to prove that the market is not free and does not satisfy wants originating with the consumers because an important sector is controlled by giant corporations, and the freedom of the market is further restricted by a large public sector controlled by governments. The dispute concerns the presence or absence of consumers' sovereignty, which is an undisputed ideal.

The idea of consumers' sovereignty raises two questions: one, are there consumers' wants of economic significance which really originate with the consuming individual, and which are not generated by his social environment? Two, does consumers' sovereignty actually lead to the satisfaction of "real" needs, and of the common good? The traditional distinction between wants that are original with consumers and wants that are created by modern advertising and salesmanship, and therefore do not originate with consumers, raises all the problems of the individualistic social philosophy of the eighteenth century: the individual is historically and structurally the primary unit; society is the product of a social contract in which individuals renounce some of their sovereignty for reasons of expediency. They retain this sovereignty in the political field through democratic institutions, and in the economic field, as sovereign consumers through "the dollar vote" in the free market. In this individualistic image of society the main problem is which political and economic system guarantees maximum individual sovereignty.

Behind this discussion, however, lies the problem of the origin of needs and wants. Modern social psychology and anthropology have shown that man was originally a social being who has only lately, in the course of modern history, emerged as an entity separated from his social ties. Even today the individual personality is influenced largely by what Erich Fromm calls the social character which makes the individual want to do what society requires him to do, and makes him want what society wants him to want. What "originates with the individual" are such physiological needs as 1,000 calories a day—otherwise he would perish; but whether they are taken in the form of steaks or rice, or three times a day at a table with silverware, or squatting around a stone bowl depends on the culture. The form in which needs and wants are satisfied is almost entirely a social creation, and the *form* of want satisfaction is economically relevant.

Advertising and salesmanship are the modern form of the

social creation of wants. In this respect they are no exception, but fit into a historical pattern; however, they involve a special kind of social creation of wants. The specific feature which distinguishes advertising from want creation in precapitalist societies is not that it originates "outside the individual" but that there is an *economic* motivation behind the social creation of these wants. In precapitalist societies, the surplus over survival needs was allocated by noneconomic institutions and political or religious elites to noneconomic goals such as the building of pyramids, temples, palaces, and so forth. Advertising is a peculiar form of the social creation of wants which is undertaken by capitalist enterprises for the sake of profits and market shares. Galbraith in *The New Industrial State* is, however, right in stating that the aims of advertising by corporate technocracies show some similarities with, for example, the aims of Egyptian priests and royal bureaucracies; the goal was (and is) perpetuation of their regime, supported by religious, political and, today, economic ideologies which they sell by image building.

In the past and today, social creation of demand required some acceptance of the ruling groups and their goals by their subjects. The Egyptian priests could not have built their temples without the population believing in the religion on which their power rested. Likewise, as Galbraith has cogently shown, the goals of the corporate technocracy—economic growth and the exercise of technical virtuosity—are socially accepted goals. The problem is not where some economists see it: in the corporate bureaucracy imposing on consumers the goal of more and more privately produced material goods and technical "progress." This "ideal" seems to be acceptable to a large proportion of the people. If consumers' sovereignty were the only issue, as economists are inclined to believe, one could say that the consumer in the modern society is almost sovereign because the giant corporations give him what he, for whatever reasons, wants to receive. Nevertheless Galbraith states: "One cannot defend production as satisfying wants if that production creates its own wants." [5] It is also true that it is im-

---

[5] *The Affluent Society*, p. 153.

possible for the consumer to escape the constant barrage of "persuasion" through advertising and that his choice is on the whole severely limited by what can be profitably standardized and mass-produced. However, all these arguments merely destroy the straw man of the sovereign consumer whose wants originate within his own person. This scarecrow was eliminated by modern advertising, assuming that it ever existed. What has been destroyed by Galbraith's arguments about the creation of wants by producers [6] is directed against this unrealistic individualistic construct which was developed to justify the free market as a government "of the people and by the people." But these arguments seem weak in view of the fact that, ever since larger organized societies existed, wants have been largely created by society; that means that they originate "outside of the individual."

This leads to the second question mentioned above: what about the "real" needs of people? What about the normative elements in human wants, the right, the good, the common good? A normative approach to the question of consumers' sovereignty, to needs and wants is required. We have described the halfhearted revival of normative thinking in economics.[7] In his *Affluent Society* (and partly also in *The New Industrial State*), John Kenneth Galbraith is a powerful protagonist of this trend. In his writings, especially in *The Affluent Society*, the renaissance of moral reasoning is obvious. There, he clearly rejects the ideal of economic growth and proposes a reexamination of the goodness or badness of more production. He believes that the increase in overall production, the increase in the Gross National Product, becomes less important in an affluent society. He criticizes the overemphasis of economics on the problem of scarcity and the problem of the "optimum allocation of scarce resources." When scarcity declines, the "optimum" or the most "efficient" allocation of scarce resources becomes less important. What becomes more important is *not how much more* is produced year by year but *what* is produced.

What Galbraith actually has done is to reintroduce moral

[6] *The Affluent Society*, chap. XI, *The New Industrial State*, chap. XIX.
[7] See above, pp. 130 ff.

questions into macroeconomics. He has raised the question of the individual and social "good." He condemns morally many of the goods produced by private industry. What is important are not Galbraith's moral judgments but the fact that he uses moral arguments in a tract on economics. The reintroduction of moral questions, indeed of questions of ultimate meaning, is a main problem in the affluent society. Galbraith's stress on the public versus the private sector involves a condemnation of the free market allocation and raises the problem of ends and of the "goodness" of economic activity. He attacks implicitly the two basic goals of industrial society: the economic growth imperative, with its ideal of an ever-increasing Gross National Product regardless of what it consists of and who gets what; and the technological imperative, demanding that everything that can be should be invented, produced and marketed regardless of detrimental consequences.

Galbraith condemns the existing value system in his doctrine of social balance and in his moral condemnation of much of our private production and consumption. In his theory of social balance he makes a moral judgment about the relative values of private goods as against social services. The latter are neglected, the former oversupplied. The general value-attitude of the majority is "that private wants are inherently superior to public wants." [8] He distinguishes necessary versus unnecessary, important versus unimportant goods and services.[9] However, he still maintains the idea of consumers' sovereignty. He concludes that the oversupply of private goods and the neglect of public wants is due to the intense advertising of the former and the absence of advertising of the latter. In other words, he seems to assume that if consumers were really sovereign, if there were no private advertising, a balance in the allocation of resources to the public and the private sectors would be established. In spite of his moral critique of our actual allocation processes, he still seems to believe that the restoration of consumers' sovereignty would remedy the situation. This is highly doubtful. What Galbraith really tries to do implicitly is to develop moral, normative standards for resource allocation and

[8] *The Affluent Society*, p. 267.
[9] *Ibid.*, pp. 147, 251.

for production and consumption which may run counter to the present attitudes of the majority of consumers who have been persuaded to accept the goals of the corporations and of the technostructure. This becomes quite clear when he condemns certain consumers' goods on moral grounds. His books abound with such moral criticism. He talks about the dangers to the quality of our lives because of the dimensions of existence which are neglected in our resource allocation. We neglect leisure, the aesthetic dimension, the humanistic aspect of life.[10] One could add that we neglect community, participation, the creation of a livable environment, and that we lack purpose and meaning in our individual and national life.

All this goes far beyond the question of consumers' sovereignty. What we are concerned with today in our preoccupation with anomie, political apathy and alienation is not consumers' sovereignty but the quality and meaning of life in a society with a fantastically high GNP and a relatively affluent majority. We are beginning to question the wisdom of this majority, *even if sovereign*, in accepting the general idea of planless, undirected economic growth and its impact on human well-being. *We are beginning to question the supreme value of consumers' sovereignty*, and to apply *objective standards of value* to economic action.

This is a legitimate return to political economy and to the times when economics was a part of moral philosophy based on objective reason—an approach which was and is appropriate whenever the ultimate meaning of economic activity is in doubt. This was the case in early capitalism and this is again the case in the affluent society. Ever since economists have pretended that economics is value-free (or value-empty), the idea of consumers' sovereignty, combined with the philosophy of the free market, has been used as an instrument in evading judgment about the goodness of the results of market allocation. This value-empty orientation has been carried into welfare economics which deals ostensibly with what is good or bad for human well-being. However, it establishes purely formal criteria of maximization without answer-

<hr>

10 *The New Industrial State,* chaps. XXVIII–XXXV.

ing the question of what kind of production and consumption actually serves to increase or diminish human welfare. Economists have been hiding behind the screen of value-empty consumer's sovereignty based on the complete relativization and subjectivization of human wants and well-being. All moral judgments and all attempts to establish objective criteria of well-being have been met with the outcry: who are you—who is Galbraith—to decide what is good or bad for me or others? This is not a valid objection against moralizing or attempts to find objective answers to what is good or bad for human beings. Such attempts and the implicit critique of existing economic goals are quite legitimate as long as one does not impose different goals by force and violence; and Galbraith (and a few others) do nothing but try to use persuasion: an eminently democratic procedure. The exclusion of a moral and cultural critique of production and consumption from economics and from the social sciences only leaves the field to the advertisers and serves to silence any doubts about the validity of the status quo. It shifts the discussion away from the moral and philosophical question of economic goals to the problem of means (free market versus corporate or governmental planning). Galbraith has broken through these inhibitions (if inhibitions they were) and this is his claim to greatness. He has reintroduced moral and ethical questions, questions of ultimate values and of the quality of life into economics. He has gone beyond consumers' sovereignty and looks for another basis for the critique of our production and consumption. The nature of this critique is also manifest in his expectation that the "educational and scientific estate" will provide leadership in the direction of improving the quality of our lives.[11] This estate is a minority, although an influential one. If they are supposed to guide the majority in reevaluating their ultimate values, the idea of consumers' sovereignty in the traditional sense as the supreme guide for economic policies is abandoned. Leadership by the educational and scientific estate becomes necessary to lead the majority of consumers in a different direction than the one we are moving now. If the value-empty

---

[11]*The New Industrial State,* chaps. XXV ff.

sovereignty of this majority were all that mattered, no change would be indicated, and the educational and scientific estate should submit to the will of the majority.

Galbraith's suggestion can be interpreted as "elitism" and as a rejection of democratic ideas about people determining their own economic goals. However, such criticism would overlook the value-emptiness and formality of the concept of consumers' sovereignty. New normative concepts are needed to distinguish between right and wrong goals of production and consumption.

In *The Economics of Welfare*, A. C. Pigou said: "But there is no guarantee that the effects produced on the part of welfare that can be brought into relation with the measuring rod of money may not be cancelled by effects of a contrary kind brought about in other parts, or aspects of welfare; and if this happens, the practical usefulness of our conclusions is wholly destroyed." [12]

The destruction of the environment through technical and economic "progress" is now well publicized by the mass media and even paid lip service to by politicians. It is significant for the "fallacy of misplaced concreteness" (Whitehead) of our age that it required fear of *external* dangers to awaken public opinion to the dangers of economic growth. Its *internal* spiritual, psychological, moral dangers, including the misallocation of resources and the reversal of all moral priorities, were insufficient to arouse public opinion.

The external dangers, however, are now well known. Demographers and ecologists have developed an apocalyptic vision of a future of real scarcity, created by the population explosion, by the limited ability of the biosphere to absorb the waste products of technology, by the "environment-destroying potential of newly developed technologies such as DDT, pesticides, etc., and by the threats of an agricultural crisis through the destruction of soil fertility and of [the] water supply." It is the total ecological equilibrium of the Spaceship Earth which is in danger. This ecological crisis will not only keep the underdeveloped nations from

---

[12] *The Economics of Welfare*, 12th ed. (London: Macmillan, 1938), p. 12.

improving their situation but "is just as disastrous for the Western nations . . . the worship in the West of a growing Gross National Product must be recognized as not only a deceptive but a dangerous avatar; Kenneth Boulding has begun a campaign, in which I shall join him, to label this statistical monster 'Gross National Cost.' " [13] In the overdeveloped West it is GNP-fetishism and in the underdeveloped part of the world the population explosion together with the ill-considered economic and technological aping of the West which threaten the survival of mankind as much as the danger of a nuclear holocaust. In view of this situation it is ridiculous to maintain that continuation of economic growth along the same lines as before satisfies human needs; catastrophic scarcity and the threat of extinction can be interpreted as need satisfaction only if one postulates a death instinct and is in favor of satisfying this urge.

Economic and technical change are inseparable from economic growth. It is highly dubious that the magnitude and pace of change in the Western economies are conducive to the satisfaction of human needs; on the contrary they continuously prevent the establishment of a satisfactory equilibrium.

There is a basic need for a balance between growth, change, dynamics on the one hand, and stability, constancy, rest, security on the other hand. This balance is disturbed by the "gale of creative destruction" in industrial society.[14] This gale and its destruction have made life in the Western economies extremely unstable. Erik Erikson once said that assimilation to the American scene involves adaptation to constant change, in itself a difficult and burdensome way of life. Kenneth Keniston considers chronic technological and economic change as one of the major alienating elements in American society.[15] The continuous change inspired by science, technology and business certainly makes life and the

[13] See Robert Heilbroner, "Ecological Armageddon," *New York Review of Books* (April 23, 1970), and P. and A. Ehrlich, *Population, Resources, Environment* (San Francisco: W. H. Freeman, 1970).

[14] Schumpeter, *Capitalism, Socialism and Democracy,* pp. 81 ff.

[15] Kenneth Keniston, *The Uncommitted: Alienated Youth in an Alienating Society* (Princeton, N.J.: Princeton University Press, 1960, 1962, 1965), chap. 8, pp. 210 ff.

future more insecure than ever. Life planning becomes almost impossible. Chosen careers and learned skills become obsolete. Even the most primitive skills such as writing and arithmetic are obliterated by typewriters and computers. Even the physical environment changes at breakneck speed. Cities and buildings are destroyed and new ones are erected within weeks. What was there yesterday is not there today. An inhabitant of New York or Chicago who was abroad for a year may have difficulties in finding his way around in the city. A psychoanalyst once defined the hometown as the place where one always knows what is around the corner. In that sense the modern urbanite has no home.

An increasingly faster rate of change is characteristic of our present economy. Although much attention is paid to the difficulties of adjustment to a rapidly changing economy, there is hardly any discussion of an optimal rate of change.[16] Is there a limit to the degree of economic change to which man can adjust? Is there a limit beyond which economic change, even if desirable in terms of more output, becomes intolerable for individuals and detrimental to well-being? It is, of course, difficult to give an answer to this question in quantitative terms; but it should be established that change is not always a gain but can inflict psychological discomfort and suffering.

The fact that statistical measurement of these psychological costs is difficult or impossible is no excuse for ignoring them. After all, economic thought made its greatest strides long before it became mathematical and statistical. The great economists from Adam Smith to Keynes based many of their findings on introspection. Insight can be used in detecting the hidden costs of economic progress. Bertrand de Jouvenel suggests the use of sensitive persons to detect the impending destructive effects of new types of production; they could be used like radar or a Geiger counter in such cases.[17]

Economic growth with its gale of destruction has contributed

---

[16] Geoffrey Vickers, *The Undirected Society* (Toronto: University of Toronto Press, 1959), pp. 73 and 114.
[17] Bertrand de Jouvenel, "The Political Economy of Gratuity," *Virginia Quarterly Review*, vol. 35, no. 4 (Autumn, 1959), p. 524.

to the alienation, insecurity and rootlessness of Western man. If he has found roots in a stable environment, economic change may uproot him again. The general feeling of insecurity and lack of community that pervades our society may stem from continuous change and its threat to physical and mental stability. The modern economy forces man into a pattern of extreme flexibility and detachment. He has to be continuously on the alert and adjust himself to the changing frontiers of production, jobs and consumption. This has made him into a lonely member of a crowd. Economic change may sever the ties of habitat and neighborhood; it may cut apart the bonds of friendship and human relations. The great attention paid to human relations in industry is a consequence of the lack of attachment and involvement that continuous change requires. Definitely there can be too much change and too fast a rate of change. Human beings require an equilibrium between change and stability, a need which is not met by the modern economy.

GROWTH-FETISHISM, INCOME DISTRIBUTION, FULL EMPLOYMENT AND POVERTY

GNP-fetishism is frequently defended as the best way to alleviate the bad effects of an unequal income distribution. Although few contend that it will abolish such inequality, it is maintained that, by increasing the GNP, everybody's share will increase and thus take the sting out of unequal incomes. This is purely quantitative, formal, value-empty reasoning which neglects the qualitative aspects of economic life. Income distribution is not purely an economic problem but also a problem of psychology, morality and justice.

Our GNP does not necessarily have to be larger but it should be more justly and *more* equally distributed. It seems that the trend toward greater equality of distribution came to a halt in the forties. Although the GNP has increased continuously, this has not achieved a sufficiently equal and fair distribution. We have to work actively toward this goal. This will require, among other things, an increase in the free services and in the formation of social capital from which the economically underprivileged benefit more than the higher income groups. This in turn will require a different allocation of resources from the one that our present mixed system has brought about. Merely advocating an increase of the GNP without a change in direction and in allocation and hoping that this will remedy the problem of unequal distribution is facile escapism.

The reason for this preoccupation with size and growth in the aggregate and for the neglect of composition and distribution is not hard to find. It is much easier and requires less revolutionary change if one confines oneself to the stimulation of the aggregate income than if one advocates policies for reallocation and redistribution. Here the congenital conservatism of economic reasoning comes to the fore. Reallocation can take place in the present circumstances only through government activity. To bring about a reallocation of resources seems to require such stringent governmental activity—taxing and spending—that few economists would dare to advocate it under present political conditions.

Another reason why economists consider growth of the GNP as a desirable policy goal is that it seems to provide a quantitative yardstick for policy decisions. Here, as so often in the modern sciences, the method determines not only the object but also the goal. The disadvantage of using GNP in policy decisions lies precisely in its purely quantitative character. Well-being depends not merely and predominantly on quantity but on quality. In respect to the GNP this means that its composition matters more than its size or its growth rate. A qualitative yardstick should be applied to national income on a wide scale. Up to now we have been plugging for more and more in the mistaken belief that this will also take care of the problem of psychologically and socially undesirable allocation. However, we should begin to ask the question: more and more of what and for whom?

An ever-increasing GNP and a continuously accelerated rate of growth is also advocated in order to bring about full employment. However, present affluence and future expected abundance have not only made doubtful the importance of continuous growth but also of full employment. Full employment is considered as a desirable economic goal for various reasons:

1. If one assumes, in line with traditional economic thought, a basic situation of scarcity of means confronted with an unlimited amount of needs and wants, it seems desirable to use all economic means and resources to the fullest to increase the total volume of production. Nothing short of full utilization of all factors of production, not only of human labor but of all land, raw materials, machines, and so forth is then indicated; anything less would be waste. This argument in favor of full employment, or better, in favor of full utilization of all human and nonhuman resources stems, as Galbraith has pointed out, from the early nineteenth-century economy of scarcity. It is less cogent in an affluent economy. If need satisfaction were all that matters, there would be nothing inherently desirable in the full utilization of resources, unless they serve to produce *needed* goods and services. If one demands a higher GNP merely to accomplish full employment, production and resource utilization become the end and consumption the means. More goods have to be produced in order to employ more people, machines and factories. More can be employed only if more goods are consumed. The natural relation between production and consumption is reversed; now it is assumed that higher production is desirable to keep factories, machines and people at work. Thus a vicious circle is created; people must consume in order to work and not vice versa. If need satisfaction is the ultimate goal, it does not make sense to increase the GNP merely to make people work; from this point of view employment is desirable only if the goods produced are needed.

2. However, another reason for the advocacy of full employment is a humanitarian one, because in our economic system employment, a job, is considered to be the appropriate reason for receiving income and purchasing power. Our Puritan economic heritage and the labor ethos make us reluctant to distribute purchasing power in the form of income except for work in traditional types of production. Those who do not work should not eat, not

only because otherwise there would be no incentive for work but also because this seems to be a principle of social justice.

However, in an affluent economy incentives for additional production along traditional lines are less urgent. Moreover, it is usually overlooked that for over a century rewards for work in production have not been the only form of income. The Western economies have used two principles for the distribution of income: achievement and ascription. Regular wages and other kinds of income are based on the principle of achievement or on contribution to production; people are paid for what they are *doing*, and "doing" is interpreted as producing. In cases of relief, unemployment compensation and the like, the basic principle is ascription: people receive income for *being*, for what they *are:* human beings in need, children, widows, and so forth. If production serves the satisfaction of needs and wants, if more satisfaction of certain needs and wants loses its importance because of affluence, more production, employment and incentives along traditional lines become superfluous. The distribution of purchasing power or income, necessary for humanitarian reasons and for moving the goods produced from producer to consumer, can then be based on the principle of ascription: crudely speaking, purchasing power and income can then be given away freely.

A trend in this direction is reflected in the many proposals for a guaranteed (minimum) income either for everybody, or, at least, for those in need. The legislation placed before Congress in 1970 provided for a family allowance plan corresponding to the structure of the economy and to our ambivalent attitude toward income: a minimum amount of income is guaranteed to the needy; this obviously because they are for social, educational and cultural reasons excluded from the mainstream of our affluence. However, they are denied help if they do not accept available jobs, a clear remnant of the labor ethic. Such schizophrenic measures would make sense if the labor power and skills, if any, of these underprivileged were needed by the economy. This was the case of the proletariat in the nineteenth century; their labor power was required but they were kept in poverty by low wages; that is, by *exploitation.* The remedy against this is the raising of wages, making them more equal to the laborer's productive contribution. Today's poor are not needed economically; they are kept poor by *discrimination.*[18] The long-run remedy against discrimination is to eliminate it; the short-run remedy is to guarantee purchasing power and income for the needy regardless of their contribution to production which is unwanted anyway.

3. However, employment and a traditional kind of job also perform a psychological function. They give meaning to life which, in Western society, is based on one's function in the economy. Work in a traditional job is considered as the only legitimate way of life. It is not only the basis of external status but also of self-respect. This invests the goal of full employment with a socio-psychological importance which transcends the purely economic arguments of incentives and purchasing power. This problem is illustrated by a story: Walter Reuther was shown a fully automated factory by Henry Ford II who said: "Walter, these machines will not pay any union dues." Whereupon Reuther answered: "But they will not buy any cars either, Henry." This story points to the old problem of technological unemployment and of the lack of purchasing power. If it were not for the psychological meaning of employment these problems could easily be solved by freely distributing purchasing power and income without requiring work which may not be available because of full automation, computerization and cybernation. The problem of income and purchasing power can be solved, but what about the need to make life meaningful, to perform a function in society, what about status and self-respect?

This is not a rhetorical or theoretical problem of a utopian future. The problem of how to separate income from traditional work and to find a new source of meaning has already arisen. It is an acute problem today for the underprivileged minorities for whom there are no jobs, but it is also a problem for the affluent majority because of the reduction in working time and the growing availability of leisure. If work becomes less and less and leisure more and more important, the source of meaning in life is shifted

---

18 Habermas, *Technik und Wissenschaft als Ideologie.*

from work to leisure. The problem will become more acute if our economy becomes more and more automated and cybernated. Serious students of automation predict that in the near future only a minority will find work.[19] According to H. F. W. Perk, in an economy in which automation, computerization and cybernation would practically shift the entire task of production to machines, such machines would provide the necessary skill, control and intelligence, leaving for man only the making of policy.[20] This would leave the majority without jobs in the traditional sense. If this should prove correct, we will have to change traditional attitudes toward work and income. This may not require that people will have to do entirely without work; but new types of activity and new ways of life will have to be developed. Income will have to be separated from holding a traditional job in producing more goods and services; and meaningful work and activity will have to be separated from jobholding. A situation may come about in which most people will have to live on an "independent" fixed income like the precapitalist aristocracy—independent from their contribution to the production of *traditional* goods and services. They may render public, therapeutic, aesthetic, artistic, entertainment, religious services the way people today engage in hobbies, and they may live on a fixed guaranteed income which is in no way related to their activity. This income they will receive even if they do nothing but enjoy themselves. Working in order to earn an ever-increasing income may even come into disrepute. People will have to think differently about income: as something that covers the necessities of life and not as something that should be escalated without end. The "dole" will have to be made respectable. It is clear that if such an attitude becomes prevalent, the moral and psychological basis for GNP-fetishism and for the desire for ever-increasing standards of living in terms of more and more income and spending would disintegrate. It also would be the end of burdensome alienated labor because nobody would be forced to pass

[19] Donald N. Michael, *Cybernation: The Silent Conquest* (Santa Barbara, Calif.: The Fund for the Republic, 1962).

[20] H. F. W. Perk, "The Great Transformation," *American Scholar* (Spring, 1966).

his time in undesirable work. It would then be possible to replace the burden of a job by activities meaningful to the person who undertakes them. Meaningful activity will have to be separated from the traditional kind of employment. Work will more and more assume the character of "play" in the sense of a meaningful end in itself. All this sounds like a dream in our present situation. However, such a glimpse into the future is not fantastic because we lack the technological means to accomplish it. The present situation can easily be described in quasi-Marxian terms: our technical productivity through automation and cybernation could make such a situation possible, even necessary, but it is prevented from doing so by our "consciousness," our attitudes toward economic activity, work and income which are involved in our individual and social growth-fetishism. Individual acquisitiveness prevents the acceptance of a guaranteed fixed income, an allocation of production according to moral and social priorities, a liberation of work through separation from income. The difference between this and the Marxian approach is that the limiting factors are our values and attitudes, that is, psychological, intellectual and spiritual factors. These conditions are of course accepted by a "ruling group," the techno-structure and the managers in corporations and government agencies; and these ruling groups have persuaded the majority to accept economic growth-fetishism. The growing movement against these attitudes not only by youth but by leading intellectuals, however, indicates that this "false consciousness" is beginning to disintegrate.

The reduction of poverty has also been used as a pretext for advocating untrammeled economic growth. This argument is open to the same objections as the one that uses full employment for the justification of growth-fetishism. If individuals in the overdeveloped economies could abandon the acquisitive attitude, the problem of poverty could be solved overnight. To use an extreme statement by Bertrand de Jouvenel: if the developed nations should decide that the living standards of the Mexican peon are more conducive to their well-being than their present hypertrophic style of life, they could not only absorb the increase in population that has to be expected but could eliminate poverty without any increase in the GNP; but one does not have to go as far as that. There are many middle ways between abject poverty and the present burdensome economic proliferation of superfluous and unhealthy goods and services.

Our ideas on affluence and poverty are interrelated. Our positive evaluation of affluence is a consequence of our concern with poverty. This concern is of a relatively recent date. It originated with the French Revolution and early capitalism. Poverty was not always regarded as an unmitigated evil. Once a certain level of subsistence and comfort is reached, evaluation of poverty depends on prevailing value-attitudes. In Christianity poverty was a virtue. Poverty and wealth are not absolute concepts, but rest on a comparison with the standard of living of others. In a rigidly organized caste society without any social mobility, even such a comparison will not lead to rebellion against poverty because everybody has an assigned place in the social hierarchy and any change is psychologically inconceivable. Such an acceptance of "poverty" was not simply imposed by a ruler but was inherent in the value-attitudes of the people. Only after the emergence of the modern industrial and mobile society did comparisons between the economic levels of the "poor" and the "rich" and the possibility of climbing upward on the income scale lead to our present condemnation of poverty and worship of affluence. The same is true today in relations between rich and poor lands. The mass media which show to the population of the poor lands the glitter and glamour of Western riches, combined with the dissolution of their traditional societies, encourage them to make comparisons and to realize that they are poor and want to be rich.

Our own hide- and culture-boundness has prevented us from studying without blinders the history and psychology of poverty and of wealth. Over and above a minimum level of subsistence and comfort, poverty is not a state of the body but a state of mind, a state of social attitudes. The *theoretically* possible evaluations of poverty and abundance range all the way from the asceticism of hermits to the love of comfort in the modern middle class, which seems burdensome to many Easterners and even to some Westerners. Everything that was said about the relativity of poverty applies equally to wealth. Affluence has become an ideal because it is the negation of poverty, and because we are condemning poverty we consider wealth as a desirable goal.

It may be, however, that the entire concept of affluence is a misconception and that this misconception stems from our traditional thinking about economic problems, and from our traditional habit of separating the economic from other human problems. Scarcity and abundance have been, and still are, looked at from the purely economic point of view; but they assume a different meaning if they are looked at from the point of view of the total human situation.

As discussed above, the *economic* concept of scarcity rests on the idea that there is only a limited supply of original factors of production, such as labor and land (for natural resources). This in itself would not necessarily lead to "scarcity" in the economic sense if it is not also assumed that this *limited* amount of factors is confronted with an *unlimited* amount of "needs." The unlimitedness of needs is an essential assumption of traditional economic theory. Limited factors and unlimited needs establish the economic scarcity which leads to justification of the production and acquisition of more and more goods as an ideal and as a way of life. The goal of economic activity is here identified with an unlimited increase in wants and a corresponding unlimited increase in production. This continuous increase in both wants and production prevents the realization of abundance in the sense of a surplus of means of satisfaction over needs. *Seen in this light abundance is an ideal which can never, and should never, be reached; the basic assumption of scarcity of means and unlimitedness of ends prevents the possibility of ever establishing complete abundance.* At the same time, the idea of abundance is also a threat to the system because, with its establishment, the entire meaning and purpose of the system—endless economic growth—would vanish.

These ideas—that abundance is an ideal and a threat at the same time—dominate the discussion of the automated and cybernated society of the future. In these discussions it is always assumed that the technological trend which will create abundance will undoubtedly continue and that nothing can and should be done about it. Being against technical progress is like being against the flag; it is taboo. But there is also the fear of abundance because it would make our economic life and system meaningless and would eliminate productive work as the only legitimate way to pass one's time.

The way out of this predicament is discussed in the next chapter. It is based on recognition that human existence and human needs are multidimensional and that abundance on one level can be accompanied by scarcity on other levels. Economics has misinterpreted the meaning of abundance by defining it as a continuous filling-up with goods and gadgets. Consequently, it has also misinterpreted poverty as the absence of such possessions. Once a subsistence and minimum comfort level is reached, a stable standard of living is not necessarily an undesirable state of affairs.

Whereas in the early 1960's there was great concern with full automation, cybernation and computerization and the problems of overabundance and leisure, concern with the ecological and environmental consequences of never-ending economic and technical growth emerged during the last years of the sixties. Obviously, there are two conflicting trends at work: either the present system will lead to overabundance and technological unemployment; or environmental destruction will enforce the end of further economic growth and technical innovation. In either case the reorientation of values we have described will have to take place. Overabundance will require a redirection of our life-style into noneconomic and nontechnical directions; and so will the ecological limits placed on further growth. In both cases we will have to abandon the acquisitive attitude, separate income from the production of more and more, and look for a meaningful life-style beyond the economic dimension.

All this should be understood as a plea for a *change in directions*, a reversal in ideals and attitudes which will have to take place to avoid the negative and the disequilibrating effects of continuous economic growth and one-dimensional abundance. It should not be misunderstood as an appeal for the return to the cave; those who are obsessed with economic growth and technological "progress" always try to discredit such warnings by carrying this counsel to the extreme of absurdity. There is a middle way between primitivism and the civilization of more and more. Everything that has been said here should be understood as an attempt to stem the dangerous tide and to point toward a *balance*, not toward a one-dimensional extreme in either way. A man is not profited if he should gain the whole world and lose his soul; nor, if he should gain his soul and lose the world.

7

Multidimensionality and the
Balance of Life

The preceding chapters have stressed the necessity for economics to include normative elements in its universe of discourse. Trends in this direction are already visible. Ideas on what is right and wrong, the good and the common good, are appearing in economic thought and are necessary for a critique of our present ideals and priorities. Such a critique will have to derive a value system from a new image of human nature.

In the first two chapters I dealt with the interrelations between alienation, repression and a central belief and value system. People cannot change their attitudes unless they become convinced that the new beliefs and values are in harmony with a higher order, with the logos of the universe, of society and of human nature. The new philosophy will have to base its critique of existing economic orientations and institutions on a concept of human nature which will show that the existing order is incompatible with essential propensities, traits, inclinations and "needs" of this nature, and that this incompatibility threatens to destroy the human substance. The economic, political and cultural ethos has to be rooted in an image of man which determines what kind of alienation and repression we will regard as inevitable and what kind we will consider unbearable.

As pointed out before, this distinction between inevitable and unbearable types of repression will also turn out to be of a dialectical historical nature. What is unbearable is the result of a historical process which has carried a one-sided life-style to the extreme so that it begins to endanger human existence and the balance of life. Such one-sidedness has to be remedied and the excessive one-directional trend reversed. The new concept of human nature will have to abandon the one-dimensional, value-empty concept of economic and technological man and create a new holistic multidimensional image. Such an image of man should tell us more than economics knows about human "needs." It is time to include a chapter on "wants and their satisfaction" in a new organon of economic thought. A new "philosophy of human well-being" is needed. I use the term "well-being" to replace the term "welfare" and the more ancient terms "happiness" and "utility" with their economic connotation. "Well-being" is related to the concept of mental and physical "health" which has a definite normative content. Modern medicine has reduced the ideal of "health" to the physiological level. What we mean by "well-being" includes the Greek ideal of "kalokagathia," the virtuous, the noble, the beautiful and the good. It consists of a synthesis of factual and normative elements and of all dimensions necessary for human existence. The concept of self-actualization, used in humanistic psychology, especially by Erich Fromm and A. H. Maslow, comes close to it if one interprets it as an all-round balanced style of life. If such a way of life is understood as a prerequisite for physical and mental health, well-being and health can be used as synonyms.

A new philosophy of human well-being will have to acknowledge that a person, a family, a group or a nation can have too much wealth and income and may suffer from too much change, economic growth and production. It may consider that the way in which wealth is produced, distributed and consumed can, in itself, lead to a destructive way of life. We shall have to develop a new discipline of human well-being which will teach people when to work and when and how to rest; when it is wise to refrain from getting more even if one can "afford" it; and how to resist the temptations of modern mass production, consumption and salesmanship should physical and mental health require it. This is not a restriction of economic freedom but the extension of a higher kind of reason into the sphere of individual existence

However, this new philosophy will have to transcend by far the limits of economics. It will have to be derived from modern ecology, biology, psychology and existential philosophy and ontology. The uniting link will have to be the idea of multidimensionality and the principle of balance between various forces, levels and dimensions. Human "well-being," including the realization of potentialities, growth and self-actualization, requires a *multidimensional balance* of existence. The elaboration of such a philosophy goes beyond the purpose of this book, but it is fitting to end it by pointing in this direction.

MULTIDIMENSIONAL BALANCE

The idea of balance stems from ecology and is widely applied today to the problems of pollution, conservation and destruction of the environment. Rachel Carson, in *The Silent Spring*, popularized this concept which has since become more and more of a militant slogan in the fight to save our natural habitat. Ecological balance refers to a situation where various "populations" (plants, animals, men) form an ecosystem, an interdependent whole which, for the purposes of survival, have to be kept in balance with each other. The elements of such an ecological balance are: (1) a multiplicity of populations; (2) a mutual interdependence of these populations; and (3) the necessity of a balance between these interdependent populations. Biologists have used this concept as the basis for a critique of untrammeled economic growth. C. H. Waddington states that "a living organism must be regarded as a nodal point in an extremely complex network of interactions, relations and transactions . . . of an internal, bio- and physio-chemical character and of external interactions with other living

184 ALIENATION AND ECONOMICS

beings and its non-living environment."[1] He approvingly quotes René Dubos who condemns "the gospel of growth—the whirling-dervish doctrine which teaches: Produce more so that you can consume more so that you can produce more still. One need not be a sociologist to know that such a philosophy is insane." One does not have to be a sociologist but one should not be an economist, because few economists do see the insanity of the growth concept.

Waddington believes that the idea of "growth" measured in merely quantitative terms of more and more goods and services produced "is influenced more by the ideas of physicists than of biologists. There is very little in the biological world—except cancer—which grows in the unrestrained way which has characterized for example the automobile industry. Normal biological growth is a well-regulated harmonious process in which all parts grow in a way that they keep pace with one another . . ." Technological growth is not like biological growth but uncontrolled in the sense that "each aspect of society increases as fast as it can with only minimal cross-reference to the situation of other parts." In the biological world almost nothing is "maximized . . . In place of maximization of entities . . . biology deals mainly with balancing, or optimization of things . . . to produce a harmonious whole; e.g. the embryo has all sorts of control mechanisms which adjust the sizes of the organs to one another . . . so that they stay in balance; or in ecological systems the number of plants and animals are . . . usually controlled . . . so that they stay in balance."[2] Biologists have criticized technical measures such as pest control, use of insecticides, water control, and so forth because, "our single-value approach conflicted with the intrinsic complexity of the environment."[3] The detrimental effects of technological measures aimed at increasing technical and economic productivity were almost entirely due to single-mindedness and one-dimensionality of purpose, which fail to consider the ecological system as an interdependent whole.

---

[1] C. H. Waddington, "A Matter of Life and Death," *New York Review of Books* (June 5, 1969), p. 32.
[2] *Ibid.*, p. 33.
[3] Barry Commoner, "Frail Reeds in a Marsh World," *Natural History*, LXXVIII, No. 2 (February, 1969), 45.

The concept of balance can also be applied to man himself, to his individual and social existence. Man can be understood as an ecosystem existing on various levels or participating in various dimensions which are mutually interdependent and have to be kept in balance. This balance can be called *existential* (in distinction from ecological) balance. The idea of an existential balance rests on the assumptions that there are various dimensions in human existence and that existential scarcity requires the balance of these dimensions during the human life-span. A hierarchical structure of human "needs" requires balanced all-round "satisfactions" of those needs, a rhythmical flow of behavior up and down this hierarchy of needs. A further assumption is that culture and society tend to alienate and estrange man from some of these dimensions by repression of some and overemphasis on others; well-being is not accomplished by pursuing one dimenison at the expense of others, but by establishing a balance between them.

There is little agreement among philosophers and psychologists about the classification of the dimensions of human existence; but there is widespread agreement that there are different dimensions, in spite of disagreement as to what they are. Paul Tillich talks about the *multidimensional unity of life*.[4] *All* life is multidimensional; and so is *human* life. Tillich distinguishes the anorganic, the organic, the spiritual and the historical (social) dimensions. These dimensions form a hierarchy; each of them is an actuality which includes potentially the "higher" dimension.

Michael Polanyi is a philosopher of science who has transcended the purely mechanistic, atomistic interpretation of science and rediscovered the importance of what he calls "personal knowledge" or intuition in scientific discovery and activity. It is significant that he has developed a classification of dimensions of being similar to that of Tillich. In *The Tacit Dimension* he establishes a hierarchy of levels. He talks about a sequence of levels found in living beings which is built up by the rise of higher forms of life from lower ones.

"The most primitive form of life is represented by the growth

---

[4] Paul Tillich, *Systematic Theology*, vol. III, pp. 12 ff.

of the typical human shape, through the process of morphogenesis studied by embryology. Next we have the vegetative functioning of the organism, studied by physiology; and above it there is sentience, rising to perception and to centrally controlled motoric activity, both of which still belong to the subject of physiology. We rise beyond this at the level of conscious behavior and intellectual action, studied by ethology and psychology; and upper-most, *we meet with man's moral sense, guided by the firmament of his standards.* These levels of human existence are above the level of the inanimate. Nevertheless, they rely for their operations on the laws of physics and chemistry. But the principle of the operations of a higher level can never be derived from the laws governing its isolated particulars; it follows that none of these biotic operations can be accounted for by the laws of physics and chemistry." [5]

Three principles are enunciated in this approach: one, the dimensions of existence form a hierarchy of lower and higher levels or dimensions; two, the higher dimension, although resting on the foundation of the lower ones, cannot be understood in terms of the principles governing the lower ones; it receives its meaning from the higher dimension which integrates the particulars of the lower dimension into a new emerging Gestalt. Three, the highest level is the dimension of the normative, of the moral sense, of the standards of value. The conclusion is that one can neither understand human existence nor lead a balanced life without taking into account *all* levels. A life-style which corresponds to the structure of human beings must involve the higher as well as the lower dimensions which are part of this structure.

In psychology, thinking along the same lines can be found in A. H. Maslow's ideas about the hierarchy of needs. [6] Maslow starts with the assumption that the human personality is an integrated whole in which every part, level and dimension is interdependent. He distinguishes physiological needs, safety needs, belongingness and love needs, and needs for self-actualization. Each

[5] Michael Polanyi, *The Tacit Dimension* (Garden City, L.I.: Doubleday & Co., 1966) pp. 36–37, italics mine.
[6] A.H. Maslow, *Motivation and Personality*, pp. 80 ff.

level or dimension generates its own needs which form a hierarchy
of relative prepotency; that means that once needs of a lower level
are satisfied, other, higher needs originating in a higher level of
existence emerge. This hierarchy of relative prepotency is another
way of talking about the multidimensionality of human existence.
What Tillich and Polanyi derive from philosophical reasoning
Maslow deduces from psychological insight. His principle of the
hierarchy and prepotency of needs is the basis of the concept of
existential balance. Man, in order to be fully alive and really
healthy, must lead a life which takes care of *all* of his needs, in *all*
of these dimensions. That does not mean complete fulfillment,
which is impossible within the limits of human mortality; but there
has to be a *balance* of satisfaction within all these dimensions.

In my discussion of alienation I distinguished between economic and existential scarcity (see above pp. 19 ff.). The real
"economic" problem is indeed created by scarcity: not the "economic" scarcity of factors of production like natural resources,
labor and capital, or the goods and services produced for sale to
others; but the *existential* scarcity of the penultimate resources of
life, time and energy, a scarcity created by our finitude and
mortality. And there is indeed in human existence a problem of
allocation of resources, not merely between what goods to produce
and to consume but how to allocate our entire life-time and life-
energy, the totality of our being, between the various dimensions
of our existence: the physis, the psyche, the spirit in its cognitive
and moral aspects, between being and becoming, contemplation and action, change and stability, affirmation and negation,
self-preservation and self-transcendence. Economists are right when
they talk about an optimum allocation problem; but the problem
is optimum allocation of life-time and life-energy to the *various
dimensions* of human existence and not only to the one economic
dimension that is involved in traditional production and consumption for and through the market. Economists are also right when
they consider such an optimum as a situation of equilibrium; but
this equilibrium has to be multidimensional, a balanced satisfaction
of needs and aspirations, in *various* dimensions, not a maximization
of one-dimensional need satisfaction. The physical, organic, psy-

chical and spiritual dimensions within a human person have to be balanced like the populations of an ecological system. To the balance of life without corresponds a balance of life within. This follows from both the multidimensionality and the finitude and mortality of human existence.

The trouble with most economic reasoning about growth is its one-dimensionality. *Economic* scarcity includes only the dimension of intentionally produced goods and services, evaluated in money and mostly for sale to others. Economic scarcity relates exclusively to things that are produced intentionally in organized production, mostly for the market. Existential scarcity includes much more: everything that human beings may need, want, desire and do, including objectives which cannot be reached by purposeful production and to which the terms production and consumption are inapplicable. There are human potentialities and needs which are not related to the procurement of goods and services and cannot be satisfied by producing and by buying and selling. Love, friendship, primary, warm, affectionate human relations; the experience of beauty, worship, the pursuit of truth and of the good, are of this nature.

These noneconomic needs which cannot be satisfied by more production for the market are *the real costs of economic growth* and of the striving for more and more goods and services. A society which allocates most of the activity of its members to the production of goods will prevent the fulfillment of other needs and aspirations. The members of such a society will consider non-market activities as inferior, less important aspects of life. Parents, peer groups, authorities and educational media instill the idea that whatever has no market value has hardly any value at all. The meaning of life in our society depends on the experience of participating in production for the market.

Economic scarcity and allocation are concerned with "material" needs and wants satisfied by organized production, whereas existential allocation and scarcity are *also* concerned with non-material, noneconomic needs and wants. Existential allocation is concerned with *every* way in which human beings pass time and use their energy.

If man is an ecosystem existing on various levels, he has to maintain a multidimensional balance. Economics has overlooked the multidimensionality of life, and has confined itself to the dimension of conscious, deliberate, intentional organized production, mostly for the market and for monetary gains. This was due to the reductionism inherent in technical economic reasoning; to the splitting off of the economic sphere from other dimensions of life; and to the quantitatively acquisitive, one-sided growth orientation which reflected the basic value system in Western society.

Economists assume that an individual will maximize his utility by "equalization at the margin" (see above pp. 84 ff.); but they apply this concept only to decisions about production for or purchase of goods in the market. What will give me more "utility": spending $10 on one more shirt or one more pair of shoes? However, this procedure can also be applied to different dimensions: too much satisfaction of material needs leaves insufficient time and energy for the satisfaction of nonmaterial needs. Continuing acquisition of money and goods takes place at the expense of all the other goals of human life. *Existential equalization at the margin requires not one-dimensional growth but multidimensional balance.* Need satisfaction which continuously increases the supply of means along one level or dimension and neglects needs on a different level is inimical to human well-being. In the ecological system that is man, the various dimensions of body, psyche, thought, spirit and morality have to grow in a balanced way; one-sided growth in one dimension throws the whole system out of gear.

ONE-DIMENSIONALITY AND ALIENATION

One-dimensionality is another term for alienation which we have defined as repression of certain aspects of human nature. The one-dimensionality of the economic orientation is a consequence of the specific form alienation took in Western society (see above pp. 36 ff.). It is a result of the reduction of reason to technical reason and of the repression of the entire "nonrational" dimension of human existence. These nonrational dimensions include the normative—values and ideals—and the emotional—feeling, passion, emotions, fantasy, imagination. They include all forms of action and expression which are related to myth and utopia. They include the spiritual dimension of thought and intuition, the realm which creates meaning. The impulse control of Western society repressed and represses not only instinctual drives but also what Keniston calls "the non-cognitive, affective symbolic stratum." Western alienation represses also nonlibidinous, nonbiological human propensities as they manifest themselves in myth, belief systems, utopias, in religious creations and transcendental experiences. Multidimensionality, then, requires the resurrection of these interrelated dimensions: (1) the *spiritual* dimension, the realm of meaning; (2) the *normative* dimension, the realm of values; (3) the *transcendental* dimension, the realm of the unknown, of the depth-dimension of existence, the realm of worship, of mystery, of faith in things unseen, of the experience of the "tremendum and fascinosum"; (4) the *affective* dimension, the realm of feelings, emotions, passions, fantasy and imagination; (5) the *communal* dimension, the realm of close relations to the other, the "thou," the realm of love.

These dimensions have been repressed and neglected in Western society. Western man has thus become alienated from important "parts" of himself because the multidimensionality of his existence has been reduced to the dimension of technology and of the economy. Western society requires the individual to choose without values (repression of the normative); to work without meaning (repression of the spiritual); to integrate without community (repression of the communal dimension). One could add: to think without feeling (repression of the affective) and to live without faith, hope, myth, utopia (repression of the transcendental dimension).[7]

To translate this into economic language: these dimensions correspond to "needs," innate in human nature, rooted in the structure of human existence; their neglect implies deprivation of

---

[7] Compare Keniston, *The Uncommitted*, p. 271.

"needs." Existential scarcity does not permit endless one-dimensional growth along purely technical and economic lines. The way out of this predicament is to strive for a new mode of life which will rectify the imbalance of Western society. But this cannot be created by external, organizational, political reforms or revolutions. Change from within is required before one can think in terms of external institutional changes.[8] Manning the barricades, even gradual social reform as advocated by liberals, is insufficient. If the goal of revolutionaries to overthrow the present "establishment" and its ruling groups were accomplished, the result would be a political system exactly like the present one unless values and attitudes have changed. A new establishment and a new "elite" *is* needed; but one with value-attitudes different from those we hold now. The revolution and the reform have to start with the individual and from within. Only individuals with a different orientation toward the values and goals of life can successfully alter the existing system; if such individuals emerge and staff the corporations, government agencies and the mass media, they could accomplish an inner revolution without great external upheavals. In this sense such a revolution will have to be individualistic and libertarian. But this libertarianism should not be confused with the economic one-dimensionality of the laissez-faire advocates whose ideas would result only in removing all countervailing power to the power of big business and of the industrial state. The new libertarian individualism will have to be in dialectical opposition to existing values and will have to strive for a multidimensional balance.

Again, it would transcend the limits of this book to elaborate in detail the way of life and the value-attitudes that would change our present institutions from within and lead to a more balanced existence. Some of the attitudes that are required have been alluded to before: abandonment of the acquisitive attitude; aiming at a "sufficient" target income; resistance to advertising and sales pres-

---

[8] The same idea is expressed by the term "revolution by consciousness" used by Charles A. Reich in *The Greening of America*, which was published after I had completed this book.

sure; prudent choice in buying with a clear idea where to stop buying; giving up the idea that forever rising standards of living are desirable.

A general simplification of life should be attempted. At present much too much time and energy are devoted not only to transportation, to getting to and from where one wants to be, and to waiting; to the filling out of forms, to red tape, to superfluous details; one has only to think of income tax returns and applications for jobs, insurance policies, and so forth. There is a fantastic waste of precious life-time for things that do not touch the substance of existence. Wherever there is a choice between making more money and simplifying life, the latter road should be taken. But much more than all this is required: abandonment of the purely activistic way of life, of getting and doing more and more for the sake of power over and control of the external world including our fellow beings; taking seriously the Kantian maxim that men should never be used as means but always as "ends"; putting more stress on being than on doing by cultivating receptivity to nature, to others, to art, to feelings; more listening rather than talking, also in relation to one's inner life; taking seriously intuition and insight by trying to resurrect what is valid in mysticism and religion; recovering the art of faith by breaking through the value-relativism of technical reason and cultivating the inner powers on which faith rests. Trends in these directions are already visible in some of today's subcultures. Whether they will prevent the destruction or dissolution which technical and economic one-dimensionality threatens to bring about and take us closer to a balanced way of life lies in the hands of fate.

Bibliography

Arendt, Hannah. *The Human Condition*. Garden City, N.Y.: Doubleday Anchor Books, 1959.

Becker, Howard. *Through Values to Social Interpretation*. Durham, N.C.: Duke University Press, 1950.

Bendix, Reinhard. *Max Weber*. Garden City, N.Y.: Doubleday Anchor Books, 1962.

Bentham, Jeremy. *Principles of Morals and Legislation*. New York: Hafner Publishing Co., 1948.

Berle, A. A. *Economic Power and the Free Society*. Santa Barbara, Calif.: Center for the Study of Democratic Institutions, 1957.

———. *Power without Property*. New York: Harcourt, Brace, 1959.

———. *The American Economic Republic*. New York: Harcourt, Brace, 1963.

———. *The 20th Century Capitalist Revolution*. New York: Harcourt, Brace, 1954.

———, and Means, G. C. *The Modern Corporation and Private Property*. New York: Macmillan, 1947.

Boulding, Kenneth E. "Economics as a Moral Science." *American Economic Review* LIX/1 (March, 1961), p. 1.

Burns, A. R. *The Decline of Competition*. New York: McGraw-Hill Book Company, 1936.

Chamberlin, Edward. *The Theory of Monopolistic Competition*. Cambridge, Mass.: Harvard University Press, 1933.

Commoner, Barry. "Frail Reeds in a Marsh World." *Natural History* LXXVIII/2 (February, 1969), p. 45.

Ehrlich, P. and A. *Population, Resources, Environment.* San Francisco: W. H. Freeman, 1970.

Galbraith, J. K. "Monopoly and the Concentration of Economic Power." *A Survey of Contemporary Economics,* edited by H. S. Ellis. Philadelphia: Blakiston, 1948.

———. *American Capitalism: The Concept of Countervailing Power.* Rev. ed. Boston: Houghton Mifflin Company, 1956.

———. *The Affluent Society.* Boston: Houghton Mifflin Company, 1958.

———. *The New Industrial State.* Boston: Houghton Mifflin Company, 1967.

Habermas, Jürgen. *Theorie und Praxis.* Neuwied am Rhein und Berlin: Verlag Luchterhand, 1963.

———. *Technik und Wissenschaft als Ideologie.* Frankfurt am Main: Suhrkamp Verlag, 1968.

Halévy, H. *The Growth of Philosophical Radicalism.* New York: Augustus M. Kelley, 1949.

Heilbroner, Robert. "Ecological Armageddon." *New York Review of Books,* April 23, 1970.

———. "On the Possibility of a Political Economics." *Journal of Economic Issues* IV/4 (December, 1970).

Horkheimer, Max. *The Eclipse of Reason.* New York: Oxford University Press, 1947.

Huxley, Aldous. *After Many a Summer Dies the Swan.* New York. London: Harper & Brothers, 1939.

Jouvenel, Bertrand de. "The Political Economy of Gratuity." *Virginia Quarterly Review* 35/4 (Autumn, 1959).

Kapp, K. William. *The Social Costs of Private Enterprise.* Cambridge, Mass.: Harvard University Press, 1950.

Kaysen, Carl. "The Social Significance of the Modern Corporation." *American Economic Review* XLVII/2 (May, 1957).

Kelsen, Hans. *Vom Wesen und Wert der Demokratie.* Tübingen: Verlag J. C. B. Mohr (Paul Siebeck), 1920.

Keniston, Kenneth. "The Sources of Student Dissent." *Journal of Social Issues* XXIII (July 3, 1967).

———. *The Uncommitted: Alienated Youth in an Alienating Society.* Princeton, N.J.: Princeton University Press, 1960, 1962, 1965.

Little, I. M. D. *A Critique of Welfare Economics:* 2nd ed. New York: Oxford University Press, 1957.

Loewe, A. *On Economic Knowledge.* New York: Harper & Row, 1965.

Loewith, Karl. "Max Weber and Karl Marx," in *Gesammelte Abhandlungen.* Stuttgart: Verlag W. Kohlhammer, 1960.

McGill, V. J. *The Idea of Happiness.* New York: Frederick A. Praeger, 1967.

Marcuse, Herbert. *Eros and Civilization.* Boston: Beacon Press, 1955.

———. *One Dimensional Man.* Boston: Beacon Press, 1964.

Marshall, Alfred. *Principles of Economics.* 8th ed. London: Macmillan, 1920.

Marx, Karl. *Die Deutsche Ideologie.* Marx/Engels Gesamtausgabe (MEGA) Erste Abteilung Band 5 Moskau—Leningrad, 1933, pp. 1 ff.

Maslow, A. H. *Motivation and Personality.* New York: Harper & Brothers, 1954.

Mason, E. S. "The Apologetics of Managerialism." *Journal of Business of the University of Chicago* XXXI/1 (January, 1958).

Matson, F. W. *The Broken Image.* New York: George Braziller, 1964.

Means, Gardiner C. *Pricing Power and the Public Interest.* New York: Harper & Brothers, 1962.

———. *The Corporate Revolution in America.* New York: Collier Books, 1964.

Michael, Donald N. *Cybernation: The Silent Conquest,* Report to the Center for the Study of Democratic Institutions. Santa Barbara, Calif.: The Fund for the Republic (1962).

Mill, John Stuart. *Principles of Political Economy.* London: Longmans Green, 1929.

Mishan, E. J. *The Costs of Economic Growth.* London: The Staples Press, 1967.

Moravia, Albert. *The Red Book and the Great Wall.* Trans. by Ronald Heine. New York: Farrar, Straus & Giroux, 1968.

Myint, Hla. *Theories of Welfare Economics.* Cambridge, Mass.: Harvard University Press, 1948.

Myrdal, Gunnar. *The Political Element in the Development of Economic Theory.* Trans. by Paul Streeter. Cambridge, Mass.: Harvard University Press, 1955.

———. *Value in Social Theory.* New York: Harper & Brothers, 1958.

———. *Beyond the Welfare State.* New Haven, Conn., and London: Yale University Press, 1960.

———. *Challenge to Affluence.* New York: Pantheon Books, 1962.

Parsons, T. *The Structure of Social Action.* Glencoe, Ill.: The Free Press, 1949.

Perk, H. F. W. "The Great Transformation." *American Scholar* (Spring, 1966), p. 366.

Pigou, A. C. *The Economics of Welfare.* 12th ed. London: Macmillan, 1938.

Polanyi, Karl. *The Great Transformation.* New York: Farrar & Rinehart, 1944, Beacon Paperback, 1957.

Polanyi, Michael. *The Tacit Dimension.* Garden City, N.Y.: Doubleday & Company, 1966.

Reich, Charles A. *The Greening of America.* New York: Random House, 1970.

Riesman, David. *The Lonely Crowd.* New Haven, Conn.: Yale University Press, 1950.

Robbins, Lionel. *An Essay on the Nature and Significance of Economic Science.* London: Macmillan, 1946.

Robinson, Joan. *The Economics of Imperfect Competition.* London: Macmillan, 1950.

Saini, K. G. "A Critique of Affluence: Mishan on the Cost of Economic Growth." *Journal of Economic Issues* 11/4 (December, 1968).

Schumpeter, J. A. *Capitalism, Socialism and Democracy.* New York: Harper & Row, 1950.

Smith, Adam. *An Inquiry into the Nature and Causes of the Wealth of Nations.* The Modern Library. New York: Random House, 1937.

Tillich, Paul. *Systematic Theology.* Chicago: University of Chicago Press, vol. I, 1951; vol. II, 1957; vol. III, 1963.

———. *My Search for Absolutes.* New York: Simon & Schuster, 1967.

Triffin, Robert. *Monopolistic Competition and General Equilibrium Theory*. Cambridge, Mass.: Harvard University Press, 1940.

Vickers, Geoffrey. *The Undirected Society*. Toronto: University of Toronto Press, 1959.

Voegelin, Erich. *The New Science of Politics*. Chicago: University of Chicago Press, 1952.

———. *Order and History*, vol. I: *Israel and Revelation*. Baton Rouge: Louisiana State University Press, 1956.

Waddington C. H. "A Matter of Life and Death." *New York Review of Books*, June 5, 1969.

Weber, Max. *Gesammelte Aufsätze zur Wissenschaftslehre*. Tübingen: Verlag J. C. B. Mohr (Paul Siebeck), 1922.

———. *General Economic History*. Trans. by F. H. Knight. Glencoe, Ill.: The Free Press, 1927, 1950.

———. *The Protestant Ethic and the Spirit of Capitalism*. Trans. by T. Parsons. New York: Charles Scribner's Sons, 1930.

Weisskopf, Walter A. "Social Anxieties and Human Conflicts." *Modern Review* II/7–8 (January, 1949), pp. 338–44.

———. "Psychological Aspects of Economic Thought." *Journal of Political Economy* LVII/4 (August, 1949), pp. 304–14.

———. "Individualism and Economy Theory." *American Journal of Economics and Sociology* 9/3 (April, 1950), pp. 317–33.

———. "Hidden Value Conflicts in Economic Thought." *Ethics* LXI/3 (April, 1951), pp. 195–204.

———. "Modern Industrialism and Human Values." *American Economic Review* XLI/2 (May, 1951), pp. 223–26.

———. "Economic Institutions and Personality Structure." *Journal of Social Issues* VII/4 (1951), pp. 1–6.

———. "The Ethical Role of Psychodynamics." *Ethics* LXII/3 (April, 1952), pp. 184–90.

———. "The Psycho-cultural Background of Adam Smith's Value Theory." *American Journal of Economics and Sociology*, 12/1 (October, 1952), pp. 63–76.

———. *The Psychology of Economics*. London: Routledge & Kegan Paul; Chicago: University of Chicago Press, 1955.

———. "The Socialization of Psychoanalysis." *Psychoanalysis* 4/4, 5/1 (Winter, 1956), pp. 52–56.

———. "Christian Criticism of the Economic Order." *Christianity and Crisis* XVI/20 (November 26, 1956), pp. 159–62.

———. "Existence and Values," in *New Knowledge in Human Values*, edited by A. H. Maslow. New York: Harper, 1958.

———. "The American Business Creed and Economic Theory." *The Journal of Religion*. University of Chicago (January, 1959).

———. "Ontology and Social Thought." *Anglican Theological Review* XLI/2 (April, 1959), pp. 105–17.

———. "The Changing Moral Temper of Economic Thought." *Zeitschrift für Nationalökonomie* XXI/1, Springer-Verlag, Vienna, Austria (1961), pp. 1–20.

———. "The Changing Meaning of Economic Action." *Festschrift für Walter Heinrich*. Graz, Austria (1963), pp. 263–75.

———. "Economic Growth and Human Well-Being." *Quarterly Journal of*

Economics and Business 4/4. Champaign, Ill.: School of Business, The University of Illinois (Summer, 1964), pp. 17–29.

———. "Economic Growth versus Existential Balance." *Ethics* LXXV/2 (January, 1965).

———. "Repression and Dialectics of History." *Review of Social Economy* XXIII/2 (September, 1965).

———. "The Psychology of Abundance," in *Looking Forward: The Abundant Society*, an occasional paper published by the Center for the Study of Democratic Institutions, Santa Barbara, Calif. (1966).

———. "Existential Crisis and the Unconscious." *Journal of Humanistic Psychology* VII/1 (Spring, 1967).

———. "Existential Balance and Evolution," in *Forum for Correspondence and Contact*, published by International Center for Integrative Studies, New York (January, 1968).

———. "The Image of Reality and the Integration of Subject and Object," in *Forum for Correspondence and Contact* I/1, published by International Center for Integrative Studies, New York (March, 1968).

———. "Alienation and Cognitive Synthesis," *Akten des XIV. Internationalen Kongresses für Philosophie*, II Vienna (September, 1968), pp. 486 ff.

———. "Mishan on Progress: A Rejoinder." *Journal of Political Economy*. University of Chicago (November-December, 1969).

———. "The Moral Problems of Modern Capitalism." *Perspectives on the Economic Problem: A Book of Readings in Political Economy*, edited by Arthur MacEwan and T. E. Weisskopf. Englewood Cliffs, N.J.: Prentice-Hall, 1970.

Worland, S. T. *Scholasticism and Welfare Economics*. Notre Dame, Ind., and London: University of Notre Dame Press, 1967.

Wössner, Jacobus. *Sozialnatur und Sozialstruktur*. Berlin: Duncker & Humblot, 1965.

Index